Sunset

BARBECUE COOK BOOK

W. FOSTER STEWART
TECHNICAL CONSULTANT

LANE PUBLISHING CO. MENLO PARK, CALIFORNIA

Library of Congress Catalog Card Number: 50–10391

FIFTH PRINTING AUGUST 1954

LANE PUBLISHING CO., MENLO PARK, CALIFORNIA

PRINTED IN U.S.A.

CONTENTS

ABOUT THIS BOOK

It takes just one or two good whiffs of the aroma of meat sizzling on an open grill, and just one or two good mouthfuls of juicy barbecued steak, to make a man want to try his own hand at barbecue cookery. And once he dons cap and apron, he is on his way to becoming a master chef.

Backyard chefs created all the recipes in this book. They are the pick of those sent in to *Sunset Magazine* over the past ten years. A glance at this assortment will show that, collectively, the barbecue expert is a nimble, versatile craftsman.

You'll find recipes to keep grill, spit, and skewers busy for many months. Here are recipes for broiling over, on, and under live coals; for roasting underground, in foil, or on a spit; for baking trout in mud, chicken in foil, tuna in gunny sacks, salmon in chicken wire. Here are three dozen savory combinations to thread on skewers for sharpening your guests' appetites; and a score of budget-balancers starring hamburger and the faithful hot dog, to alternate with 14-carat steaks. You'll find recipes to feed 300 guests, for a crowd of 25, for your family, for just yourself. There is also a challenging assortment of sauces that range from the simple button-of-garlic-in-oil to lengthy formulas that sweep the spice shelf clean.

Experts enlarge the scope of barbecuing beyond broiling and roasting over open coals. For variety, they set a large skillet or a heavy kettle on the grill and load it with stew, hash, vegetables, goulash, game, or what-have-you. In the chapter of skillet and kettle recipes are side dishes to accompany broiled meats, hearty outdoor dishes that stand on their own four feet, and some recipes that ennoble inexpensive cuts of meat.

The chef makes good use of his oven—whether it be Spanish-Mexican-Indian-Italian-beehive, portable tinplate, or kitchen range—to yield substantial pastas, bean mixes, or meat casseroles with built-in barbecue flavor. Many of these dishes are started indoors, finished outside.

A short chapter of salad recipes gives recognition to the fact that the best possible complement to flavorsome meat is a crisp, cool salad, skillfully torn and tossed, deftly seasoned.

The final chapter contains a discussion of basic barbecuing technique and a set of two dozen menus. Veteran chefs may find this part old-hat, or at least something to disagree with. The apprentice barbecuer, it is hoped, will find it helpful.

BROILING ON THE GRILL

BEEF

STEAK WITH GARLIC OIL

Steak (12 oz. to 1 lb. per person)
2 cloves garlic
1 cup olive oil

Put the garlic to soak in oil the night before the barbecue. Have meat cut from ¾ to 1 inch thick and gashed around the edge about every 4 inches so it won't curl during grilling. Pour the oil into a shallow pan, remove the garlic and dip the steak in the oil, coating both sides. Then place the steak on the grill. When it is about done, season it with salt and pepper.

TOP O' THE MORNING STEAK

Steak, medium thick
Olive oil
Salt
Onion salt
Garlic salt
Bay leaves
Pepper, freshly ground

Paint the steak on both sides with olive oil. Sprinkle liberally with seasonings, place on the grill, and cook as desired. Just before removing the meat, quickly burn a spray of bay leaves under one side and then the other.

BRANDY-BROILED STEAKS

About 15 minutes before you get ready to barbecue steaks, sprinkle both sides of the steaks generously with California brandy. Then let them stand in a crock or an enamel plate. Broil over coals; and when nearly done, salt both sides to taste.

STEAK HAWAIIAN

- 1 clove garlic
- ½ to 1 cup soy sauce
- Steak

Chop the clove of garlic very fine and put it in a large shallow glass baking dish or platter. Add the soy sauce and mix. Marinate your steak in this sauce for about 15 minutes, turning it frequently to thoroughly impregnate the meat with the seasoning. Then barbecue to taste. Do not marinate in a metal utensil as it may affect the flavor. Marinade may be used for other meats.

STEAK MARCHAND DE VINS

- 2 tablespoons chopped shallots
- 1 cup dry red wine
- ¼ pound butter
- 1 teaspoon chopped parsley
- 3 tablespoons very thick soup stock
- A few drops of lemon juice
- Salt and pepper
- Beef marrow
- 4 porterhouse steaks, 1½ inches thick

Put the chopped shallots and the wine in a wide saucepan and cook until the total volume has been reduced by more than one-half; let cool. Then cream this wine and shallot mixture into the butter, along with the parsley, soup stock, lemon juice, salt, and pepper. The marrow should be poked from 2-inch sections of beef leg bone and poached in salted water for 1 minute before slicing. (If you have a passion for marrow, you'll spread some on a piece of toast, salt it lightly, and slip it under the broiler for a minute, which produces a delicacy to munch on while you're completing the sauce.) Grill the steaks over a wood fire (use dried grape shoots if possible). At the moment of serving, strew small pieces of beef marrow over the steak and pour the sauce over all. Enough sauce for 4 good-sized steaks. This is a true Bordelaise sauce. It's also excellent on broiled lamb, or mutton chops, and on grilled mushrooms, or liver.

SALT-BROILED STEAK

This steak must be boneless, lean meat, from 2 to 3 inches thick. Use a large double grill, or toaster, with long handles that loop

together. Place the steak on the grill and cover the top with about half an inch of thoroughly dampened coarse salt (not rock salt). Then put a paper napkin over it. Turn the grill over and cover the other side of the steak in exactly the same way. Close the toaster and put it over a very hot charcoal or wood fire, allowing from 15 to 20 minutes for each side. Melt 1 or 2 pounds of butter in a large roasting pan and have ready sliced bread (preferably French). When the steak is done, remove the salt, now a hardened cake. Lift the steak into the hot butter and slice downward so you can regulate the thickness. The meat juices will run into the butter—the salt flavor will not go into the meat. With a fork, dip a slice of the bread into the melted butter and meat juices. Place a slice of beef on each piece of bread. Serve immediately.

STEAK SANDWICH

Chives
Butter
Small filet steaks, ¼ inch thick

Chop chives fine and mix in melted butter. Place steaks on grill and brush frequently with butter-chives mixture. A few minutes before the steaks are done, toast bun halves on the grill. Butter buns and serve steaks between the halves.

SNOQUALMIE STEAK

¼ cup butter (½ cube)
1 clove garlic, chopped fine
1 teaspoon seasoned salt
¼ teaspoon Worcestershire sauce
Top sirloin steak, 1½ inches thick

Melt butter. Mash garlic and salt together; add to butter with paprika and Worcestershire sauce. As it broils, swab the upper side of the steak with the mixture. Turn the steak about four times during the cooking; and swab each time with the butter mixture. While the steak is cooking, slice 6 or 8 wiener rolls in half. Serve up the steak with potatoes that have been cubed raw, unpeeled, and fried with onions in salad oil. Then, paint the rolls with the remaining sauce and toast them over the coals. Incidentally, over a forest camp stove, the slower and smokier the fire, the better the steak. Enough sauce for 4 servings. Figure on ⅓ pound steak per person.

SLICED SIRLOIN

Instead of individual steaks, try serving your guests ½-inch slices of sirloin, cut from a 2½-inch steak broiled over the coals. Serve with melted butter.

BOOLKOKI

This Korean dish, pronounced "Bullgogi," is usually served with plain boiled rice, a cabbage salad, and fruit dessert.

- 3 pounds lean beef (chuck, sirloin tips, or steak)
- 1 cup salad oil
- ¼ cup sugar
- 2 tablespoons soy sauce
- 4 tablespoons finely chopped green onion
- 2 cloves garlic, minced
- ½ teaspoon salt
- ½ teaspoon pepper
- 4 tablespoons sesame seed

Cut beef in rather thin slices or strips. Mix remaining ingredients and pour over meat. Be sure that meat is well covered with sauce. Let stand overnight in refrigerator. Take out and bring to room temperature. When ready to broil over hot coals, drain off surplus sauce. Cook on narrow-mesh grill or else thread on skewers. Baste with sauce as necessary during broiling. Serves 6.

BEEF SHORT RIBS

Two days before the barbecue purchase 6 pounds of beef short ribs cut about 3 inches long. (This will serve 8.) Marinate the meat for 48 hours in the following mixture:

- 1 No. 2 can (2½ cups) tomato juice
- 1 tablespoon sugar
- 1 teaspoon Worcestershire sauce
- ¼ teaspoon each: ginger and allspice
- 1 teaspoon celery salt
- ½ cup vinegar

Put in the refrigerator and turn the meat frequently. For the last 4 hours, remove from the refrigerator and add 1 finely-chopped onion and a cut clove of garlic.

Remove the meat from the marinade, and pot-roast it in a Dutch oven on top of the stove or in a covered roasting pan in the oven. Use a minimum of water, and keep the heat low. When almost tender, take out and complete cooking on the grill. Baste with basting sauce described below until brown and slightly crisp. Serve with sauce.

While meat is cooking, strain marinade, discard onion and garlic. Mix ½ cup of marinade with ¼ cup of olive oil or drippings to baste the meat while barbecuing. Use the rest of the marinade to make the following sauce to serve with the meat: Sauté a finely chopped onion until brown; add the marinade and 1 teaspoon each of powdered oregano and cumin. If these are not available, substitute 2 teaspoons of chili powder. Boil the sauce down until it is about half the original volume.

Here's a simpler recipe that serves 4:

- 3 pounds short ribs of beef
- 2 tablespoons prepared mustard
- ¼ cup vinegar
- ¼ teaspoon black pepper
- 1 cup canned tomato juice
- 1 teaspoon salt
- ½ tablespoon sugar

The day before meat is to be served, pack into a bowl. Beat the other ingredients together, and pour over the meat. Cover and let stand overnight. Put drained meat on grill; cook slowly, turning meat about every 15 minutes.

RIB STEAKS

When barbecuing rib steaks, pound finely minced or crushed garlic into the steaks. Cover with wine vinegar; let stand for several hours at room temperature. Drain and grill.

CHUCK ROAST

- 2 cloves garlic, finely minced
- 2 tablespoons olive oil
- ¼ teaspoon dry mustard
- 1 teaspoon soy sauce
- ½ teaspoon rosemary, crushed, or 1 sprig of the fresh herb
- 2 tablespoons wine vinegar
- 4 tablespoons Sauterne
- Chuck roast, 2½ to 3 inches thick
- 2 tablespoons catsup
- ½ teaspoon Worcestershire sauce
- 1½ teaspoons A-1 sauce

Sauté garlic gently in olive oil, add mustard, soy sauce, and rosemary. Remove from fire and stir in vinegar and wine. Pour this sauce over roast in a bowl, and cover. During the next 24 hours, turn the meat frequently in the sauce. Prior to barbecuing remove the meat and to the remaining sauce add the catsup, Worcestershire and A-1 sauces. Stir well and apply some to meat before barbecuing; continue using as a basting sauce during cooking. If the sauce appears too thick, add more olive oil. The meat should be turned frequently and basted often. A piece of meat 2½ inches thick should be cooked over hot coals for 40 minutes. When served it will be charred outside, rare in the middle. Serves 4 to 6.

HAMBURGER

BEAN-BURGER

Place grilled hamburger on toasted bun or French bread slice which has been spread with garlic butter. Top with a generous spoonful of chili beans.

SWEET-SOUR HAMBURGER

For a change try this: Place slice of raw sweet onion on top of grilled hamburger and cover with sugar.

SMOKY HAMBURGERS

Broil hamburger patties on each side. Place on lightly toasted bun spread with smoke butter, made by blending ¼ cup of soft butter or margarine with ⅛ teaspoon liquid smoke. Top with thin slices of tomato and onion, and a few mushrooms that have been sliced and sautéed in butter.

Variation:

- 1 pound ground beef
- ½ teaspoon liquid smoke
- 1 egg
- Salt and freshly ground pepper

Add the liquid smoke and the egg, beaten, to the meat; season, and mix thoroughly. Form in cakes and broil.

GROUND ROUND AND MARROW

Have a pound of top round steak passed through the grinder three times with a quarter pound of marrow. As this comes from the machine, together with the natural wrapping from the butcher, it will have the correct cylindrical form. When ready to cook, just cut a thick, liberal slice and place it upon the grill. The marrow will give it a natural flavor and will practically eliminate the necessity for condiments and sauces.

HAMBURGER CAKE

Shape seasoned meat into large round cake. Grill over coals, brushing surface with your favorite barbecue sauce during the grilling. Cut into pie-shaped wedges and serve between scones or buns.

GROUND FLANK

- 1 pound lean steer flank
- ¼ pound steer kidney suet
- ¼ teaspoon garlic salt
- 1 teaspoon salt
- ½ teaspoon each sugar and black pepper
- 2 tablespoons onion juice
- ¼ teaspoon Tabasco sauce

Grind meat through medium grinder, running it through only once. Mix in other ingredients thoroughly, but lightly, and form into a rectangle about 3 by 6 inches. Place between two pieces of waxed paper and roll lightly with a rolling pin to about ½-inch thickness. Cut into 6 portions, about 2 by 3 inches, and grill.

HAMBURGER WITH MILK

2 pounds ground beef
1 egg
¾ cup milk
Chopped onion
Pinch of marjoram and mace
Salt and freshly ground pepper

Break the egg on the meat, add the milk and seasonings, and mix and knead well before forming into balls or one large hamburger. While broiling baste with a sauce made from:

3 parts olive oil
1 part red wine or wine vinegar
Trace of thyme and garlic
Pinch each of sugar, dried marjoram, and rosemary

HAMBURGER ON THE LEAN SIDE

1 pound ground beef
Salt and freshly ground pepper
A dash of meat sauce
½ teaspon curry powder
½ jigger cognac
1 egg
1 small can chopped mushrooms
Chopped onions
Olive oil

Trim every trace of fat from the meat before putting it through the grinder. Season with salt, pepper, meat sauce, curry powder, and cognac. Add the raw egg, mushrooms, and the chopped onions that have been fried to a delicate golden brown in olive oil. Form meat into generous cakes and broil.

POTATO HAMBURGER

1½ pounds ground beef
3 medium-sized unpeeled raw potatoes, diced
1 small onion, chopped
2 tablespoons chopped parsley
Salt and pepper

Mix together the meat and the potatoes, run through the food grinder, skins and all. Add the chopped onion and parsley; salt and pepper to taste. Shape into medium-sized patties and broil. Serve without sauce.

For variety, fry in skillet. Brown flour in the pan juices after frying the patties, add milk, and season with salt and pepper, making a thick milk gravy. Pour the gravy over the patty and serve. A delicious quick gravy can be made by emptying a can of condensed mushroom soup in the cooking pan and thinning slightly with milk.

HAMBURGER HOT DOGS

Form ground meat into shape of hot dogs. Barbecue as usual. Serve in hot dog rolls with relishes.

STRETCHED HAMBURGER

1 pound ground beef
2 carrots, grated
2 pieces celery, grated
1 sprig parsley, finely chopped
1 green pepper, finely chopped
1 onion, finely chopped
1 clove garlic, finely chopped
1 tablespoon steak sauce
1 egg
Dash salt and pepper
2 tablespoons cooking oil or shortening
8 or 10 hamburger buns
½ cup melted butter or margarine

Mix all ingredients together well, using egg as binder. Roll into patties the size of hamburger buns and broil until rare, medium, or well done. Split hamburger buns into halves and toast cut sides, then brush with melted butter. Cover each hamburger with one slice of beefsteak tomato and several slices of fresh, crisp, unpeeled cucumber. A little prepared mustard may be added, if desired.

BURGERS FOR THIRTY

Form 10 pounds of ground beef into patties. Salt and pepper the hamburgers as they are placed on the grill and brush with the following sauce as they broil:

4 tablespoons olive oil
Chopped onion to taste
1 cup chili sauce
1 cup catsup
2 tablespoons dry mustard
2 tablespoons Worcestershire sauce
1 cup wine vinegar
6 tablespoons brown sugar
1 cup water
Savor salt

Put oil in a skillet, add chopped onion to taste, and brown. Add chili sauce, catsup, mustard, Worcestershire sauce, vinegar, brown sugar, and water. Sprinkle with savor salt and let simmer for 15 minutes.

HAMBURGER IN TOAST

1½ pounds ground beef
½ cup finely chopped yellow cheese
1 tablespoon minced onion
¼ teaspoon salt
¼ teaspoon mixed celery and garlic salt
Dash of Tabasco sauce

Mix well and shape into square cakes the size of a slice of sandwich bread. Brush with bacon drippings and broil.

Toast white sandwich bread, butter while hot, and stack on cookie sheet at back of grill. Lay finished hamburger upon a slice of prepared toast and pour about a teaspoon of hot barbecue sauce over it. Top with toast and serve immediately.

BEEF AND GRASS

1 egg
1 pound ground beef
1 handful each of finely-chopped spinach and watercress
1 tablespoon chopped onion
½ teaspoon paprika
Salt and freshly ground pepper

Break the egg over the meat, add the spinach and watercress, chopped onion and seasonings and work together until well blended. Then broil on the grill. NOTE: Chopped oysters can also be added to the formula; parsley substituted for watercress.

GLORIFIED HAMBURGER

1 pound ground beef
1 cup cracker crumbs
1 cup tomato juice
1 egg
1 small onion, finely chopped
Salt and pepper to taste

Mix these ingredients together and form in patties.

FRENCHMAN'S LOAF

Split lengthwise large heated French roll. Spread with garlic butter. Cover bottom half, overlapping small, thin, broiled hamburger patties, with cheese, onion, tomato, and pickle slices. Sprinkle with salt and chili sauce. Add a little finely chopped crisp lettuce and cover with top of roll. Press down firmly. French bread may be used in the same way, cutting the loaf in 4 or 5 pieces.

HAMBURGER DE LUXE

Press ground beef into very thin, flat cakes between waxed paper. Put two cakes together with a filling made from finely chopped raw onion mixed with steak sauce, crimping the edges of the cakes firmly together. Broil over the coals and serve in hot picnic buns, split and buttered. Cheese slices may be substituted for the onion filling.

HAMBURGER DOUGHNUTS

Pat out seasoned meat and cut rounds with a doughnut cutter. Grill over coals in usual manner. Serve on buns, filling the center hole with relish or melted cheese.

LAMB

GYPSY LAMB

Before barbecuing a roast of lamb or chops, rub with salt in which garlic has been mashed. Then place a layer of onion in the bottom of a pan or crock. Put in the meat and pile sliced lemon and sliced onion on top and around sides. Cover and let stand in cool place overnight, or longer if possible. Before cooking, shake plenty of paprika over the meat. The lamb is then ready to be roasted or grilled.

LAMB CHOPLETS

For lamb choplets (stuffed lamb chops), have butcher remove breast bone from breast of lamb. Cut away first 2 or 3 ribs from point end of breast and remove boneless flank end. Cut meat and some fat from trimmings and, with an extra pound of shoulder meat, grind in food chopper. Season with salt, pepper and ½ teaspoon mace. Then make a pocket in breast and stuff tightly with ground meat. Chill, cut between ribs, and grill over hot coals.

GROUND LAMB WITH PINEAPPLE RING

Onion juice, lighter and gentler than chopped or grated onion, is used to flavor this lamb dish. The method of extracting onion juice is worth noting for use in other recipes.

1 large onion, minced
1½ teaspoon salt
1 pound ground lamb
2 stalks celery and leaves, chopped very fine
4 rings of pineapple
Paprika

Place onion in a small bowl, sprinkle with salt, and let stand for about ½ hour. Turn onion onto a square of cloth, roll it up, and twist ends to squeeze out onion juice over ground lamb. Add celery and leaves to meat; work with hand to mix well. Divide into 8 portions, then form each into a roll about 3 inches in length. Place meat on the grill and broil until nicely browned. Place pineapple rings on grill and sprinkle them generously with paprika; put on grill during last 10 minutes of cooking. Makes 4 servings.

LAMB BREAST, SHANKS

Either lamb breast or lamb shanks may be barbecued with rewarding success. Lamb breast may be placed directly on the

grill, but lamb shanks should be precooked until tender before grilling. Braise shanks in small amount of water in a stout, covered pan.

Marinate 4 pounds lamb breast or 4 to 6 pounds precooked shanks in:

- 1 cup orange juice
- ½ cup lemon juice
- 2 tablespoons sugar

For last 2 hours, add ½ cup of chopped, crushed mint leaves to marinade.

Oil the meat well, place on grill over slow fire, and cook until thoroughly browned. While cooking, baste with a sauce made of ½ cup of the marinade mixed with ¼ cup of salad oil. Heat remainder of the marinade and serve as a sauce with the meat.

LAMB CHOPS

This method gives not ordinary barbecued lamb chops, but delicious small "lamb roasts" for each guest. The meat selected is a split loin of lamb—preferably hung for 8 to 10 days at the market before barbecuing. Have the butcher divide the split loin into about 6 chops, cutting through the bone but not completely separating the cuts. In this way the whole large piece can be cooked as one roast, yet easily divided into large loin chops for serving. Rub the meat lightly with a cut clove of garlic, then roast on the grill over glowing coals. Turn as frequently as necessary for even cooking, and baste with a favorite barbecue sauce or not, as desired. Ordinarily 40 to 45 minutes should be long enough to allow for the roasting. Then, with a sharp knife, divide into chops and allow one for each serving. A half rack of lamb may be barbecued in the same way if you want to use the rib cut instead of the loin.

PORK

GRILLED BACON

The best results are obtained by buying part of a side of bacon and having it sliced somewhat thicker than is customary. If there is a large crowd, the bacon should be first sliced and then replaced in its original block form and put into a bread pan. This is placed in the oven for 15 minutes at medium heat. In that way much of the surplus fat is removed, which reduces the possibility of flare-ups in cooking the bacon. Then place the bacon strips, separated, on the grill over a slow fire and cook, turning once or twice, until done.

ROASTED SAVORY SPARERIBS

Select as many sides of spareribs as required and have the butcher crack them down the middle. Cut between the ribs into serving-size pieces. Rub each piece well with a mixture of 2 tablespoons rubbed sage to 1 cup flour.

Place the ribs over charcoal fire and cook slowly for 45 minutes to 1 hour, depending on the thickness of the ribs and the heat of the fire. Turn frequently and swab often with a sauce made by combining the following ingredients:

- 1 teaspoon garlic salt
- 1 teaspoon onion salt
- ½ teaspoon freshly ground pepper
- 1 teaspoon seasoning salt
- 1 teaspoon dry mustard
- ½ cup olive oil
- ½ cup vinegar
- 1½ cups cold water

SPARERIBS WITH ONION

- Sweet onions, chopped fine
- Pork spareribs, cracked
- Salt and pepper
- Butter to sauté onions

Spread finely chopped onions on spareribs, roll up with onions inside and place in refrigerator or cooler overnight. Just before barbecuing, scrape off onions and season meat with salt and freshly ground pepper. Onions should be sautéed in butter and served with spareribs. No barbecue sauce required.

EASY RIB-BARBECUE

Select meaty lamb breast or pork spareribs and cut in pieces. Place between wire toaster. Cook about 5 inches above bed of coals. Grill for 25 minutes, turning every 5 minutes, then brush with barbecue sauce and continue grilling for 10 to 15 minutes longer. Ribs may also be conveniently cooked in a revolving grill or on a spit.

SEASONED SPARERIBS

- 5 pounds spareribs
- 1 teaspoon salt
- ⅛ teaspoon pepper
- 1 lemon, sliced thin
- ½ cup minced onions
- 1 teaspoon chili powder
- 1 teaspoon celery salt
- ¼ cup wine vinegar
- ¼ cup Worcestershire sauce
- 1 cup catsup
- 2 cups hot water
- ¼ cup brown sugar
- Dash of Tabasco sauce
- 1 ginger root sliced thin

Place spareribs on grill rounded side up, sprinkle with salt and pepper, arrange lemon slices over ribs. Baste with sauce made of remaining ingredients. This can also be cooked in the oven: bake it for 45 minutes at 450°, then 45 minutes at 350°. Serves 6.

PORK SPARERIBS

¼ cup brown sugar
1 tablespoon salt
1 tablespoon celery seed
1 tablespoon chili powder
1 teaspoon paprika
2 to 3 pounds pork spareribs
¼ cup vinegar
1 cup canned tomato sauce or puree

Mix the dry ingredients and rub part of the mixture into the ribs. Combine what is left with the vinegar and tomato sauce for basting. Let ribs stand an hour or longer, if convenient, then spread on grill over slow fire, basting occasionally with sauce. To reduce cooking time, pre-cook ribs in kitchen oven until almost tender, then finish on barbecue grill. Serves 3 or 4.

SMOKY SPARERIBS

3 pounds pork spareribs
Liquid smoke
1 clove garlic
1 onion
Few sprigs parsley
Salt
Pinch each of rosemary leaves, ginger, and coarsely ground black pepper
½ cup dry Sherry
2 tablespoons tomato paste
2 tablespoons sugar

Cut ribs into serving pieces and swab generously with liquid smoke. Place in a shallow open baking pan. Chop garlic, onion, and parsley together until fine; toss over meat. Sprinkle with salt, rosemary leaves, ginger, and pepper. Cover pan with waxed paper and let stand overnight. When ready to cook, remove from pan and grill over a slow fire. Mix Sherry, tomato paste, and sugar, and use for basting sauce. Grill until ribs are well browned and meat is tender, basting frequently with sauce. Serves 3 to 4.

SPICY SPARERIBS

2 pounds spareribs
1 can (8 oz.) tomato sauce
4 whole cloves
⅛ cinnamon stick
1 stalk celery, chopped fine (or ¼ teaspoon celery salt)
1 clove garlic (or ¼ teaspoon garlic salt)
2 dashes Tabasco sauce
1 tablespoon steak sauce
2 tablespoons vinegar
1 tablespoon sugar
½ teaspoon chili powder
2 tablespoons chutney
⅛ teaspoon dry mustard
1 small onion, chopped fine

Leave ribs in one piece. Cook all other ingredients for 20 minutes or until blended to taste. While barbecuing ribs, keep well basted. Serves 2.

HAM WITH PINEAPPLE SAUCE

Broil thin slices of ham on the grill. When slightly brown, begin basting with pineapple sauce and continue until ham is tender and well seasoned.

Basting sauce is made with the following ingredients:

1 cup brown sugar
½ cup vinegar
2 tablespoons dry mustard
1 cup pineapple juice

Cook the sugar, vinegar and mustard together slowly for 3 minutes. Remove from the heat and add the pineapple juice.

SPARERIBS ENCINO

Cut 6 pounds lean pork spareribs into individual-sized servings. Broil over coals in barbecue, until golden brown. Brush with barbecue sauce (see below). Place in covered roasting pan and let steam on back of the barbecue grill for at least one hour. Do not allow ribs to dry out. Baste frequently with sauce and fat from bottom of roaster. Serves 6.

The sauce is made from the following ingredients:

2 large onions, minced
2 tablespoons olive oil
8 large, ripe tomatoes
1 green pepper, sliced
¼ cup chopped celery leaves
1 pinch each: sage, oregano, thyme, rosemary, sweet basil
Salt and pepper to taste
2 tablespoons white wine vinegar
Sherry wine

In a large saucepan, sauté onions in olive oil until transparent. Quarter tomatoes and add to onions with green pepper, celery leaves, herbs, salt, and pepper. Cover and simmer slowly until tomatoes are soft. Put mixture through a coarse sieve to remove tomato seeds and other solids. Return mixture to stove, add vinegar, and let simmer to a thick paste, stirring frequently. When ready to use, dilute with ¾ cup Sherry to ½ cup of barbecue paste. The paste may be made ahead in quantities and sealed in jars or bottles.

BARBEMUSH APPETIZER

1 pound salt pork, diced
3 or 4 large onions, minced
1 clove garlic, minced
4 cups water
1 tablespoon chili powder
½ teaspoon oregano
½ teaspoon cumin seed
2½ cups yellow cornmeal
¼ cup sliced green olives

The day before the barbecue, fry the salt pork slowly until crisp; sauté onions and garlic in the drippings until golden; set aside.

Put water in the top part of a double boiler and bring to a boil; add seasonings and gradually stir in the cornmeal; cover and cook over boiling water for about 45 minutes. When done, add salt pork, onions, and olives. Turn out into a well greased square pan that will give ample slices. Let stand until the next day.

An hour before barbecuing meat, grill well-oiled ½-inch slices of the cold mush over a fairly hot fire. The slices will lose moisture and shrink, and when thoroughly done and crisp, will let go of the grill so they can be turned easily. Cook till crisp, and if slightly scorched, so much the better. Tier them up on the side of the grill while cooking the meat.

PERRO CON QUESO

Here's a novel way to cook the ever-faithful hot dog: Take any quantity of frankfurters (the short, chubby ones are best) and core them with a piece of thin-wall, ⅜-inch copper tubing, that has been sharpened at the cutting end. Cut strips of cheese ⅜-inch square, and stuff in the hole. Grill until the frank is cooked and the cheese melted inside. Serve in toasted hot dog rolls. The frankfurter cores have to be punched out of the tubing with a stick. Chop them up and add them to a fresh garden salad.

FOWL

BARBECUED CHICKEN

Use young chickens weighing 1½ to 2 pounds. Have them cleaned at the market, and split for broiling. Broil halves on the grill over a bed of coals, cooking inside first, skin side last. Use hinged double rack or revolving grill. Baste frequently with this sauce:

- ⅔ cup butter
- ⅔ cup hot water
- 2 teaspoons A-1 sauce
- 1½ tablespoons lemon juice
- ¼ teaspoon Tabasco sauce
- 2 teaspoons sugar
- 1 teaspoon salt
- A few grains cayenne
- 2 teaspoons flour

Melt the butter and add the water and other liquids. Blend the dry ingredients and stir into the liquid, stirring well. Cook for 2 or 3 minutes or until the mixture thickens slightly.

Some cooks prefer to soak chickens in California olive oil, with a liberal seasoning of coarsely ground black pepper, for 4 or 5 hours before barbecuing in this way.

CHICKEN

Cut 3 frying chickens into pieces as for frying. Brush with melted butter, and place over coals for about 5 minutes to sear, and then turn. Brush with sauce and turn every 3 to 5 minutes, brushing with sauce at each turn. Time required is about 45 minutes. Serves 6.

Basting sauce is made with:

- ½ cup white apple vinegar
- ⅓ cup salad oil
- 1½ teaspoons Worcestershire sauce
- ½ teaspoon minced onion
- 1 clove garlic, minced
- 3 teaspoons salt
- 1 teaspoon paprika
- 1½ teaspoons tomato paste
- 6 to 8 drops Tabasco sauce
- ¼ teaspoon dry mustard

Best to make the sauce at least 24 hours before using.

BARBECUED CHICKEN, PAPRIKA

- 2 fryers or broilers (about 1½ to 2 pounds)
- 2 cups olive oil
- 2 or 3 cloves garlic, well minced
- 4 heaping tablespoons paprika
- Salt and pepper

Quarter, wash quickly, and dry chicken well; place in shallow pan. Mix together the oil, garlic, and paprika, then pour over chicken. Marinate for 3 to 4 hours, turning the chicken about every half hour. Season with salt and pepper and place quarters on grill. Broil over hot coals, baste frequently with the marinade. Serves 4.

TURKEY STEAKS

Here's a recipe that will leave your butcher shaking his head in disbelief and will stir your guests into pelting you with questions:

Buy a large, hard frozen, eviscerated tom turkey—the bigger the better. Have your butcher cut it on his power saw, into 1-inch transverse slices, starting at the front of the breast bone, and working back to about where the thighs join the body. If you're serving a large number of people, have him cut more slices—one slice will make two good servings. The two ends that are left can be kept frozen until you need them.

Now lay the frozen slices out in a large flat pan (you can stack them) and drizzle on enough cooking oil to coat each one. As they thaw, the oil and the turkey juices will make a fine marinade in the pan. This should be brushed back over the slices from time to time. When they are completely thawed, divide

each slice into two steaks with a sharp, heavy knife. (You'll find that the cross-sections of breast and backbone will split easily.)

Have a good, hot bed of coals going in the barbecue. Arrange the steaks in toasting racks, brush with basting sauce (1/4 pound butter, 1/2 cup dry white wine, salt, and pepper). Broil about 8 inches from the fire for around 10 minutes on each side. Turn them a couple of times during the cooking, and brush with more butter-wine mixture.

Serve them up, one to a customer, with the remainder of the basting sauce heated and spooned over each serving, and have the guests guess what they're eating. You'll get quite a variety of answers—from pork, veal, to swordfish. The steaks don't taste like the customary roast turkey, but you'll agree that it is some of the best turkey you ever sank a tooth into. Once again, not too much cooking. Don't let them dry out.

YOUNG TURKEY

1 6 to 9 pound broiling turkey
Salt and pepper
1 cup favorite barbecue sauce
Dash liquid smoke

Cut turkey in pieces as you would a frying chicken and lay in roasting pan. Sprinkle lightly with salt and pepper, and cover with sauce made by combining remaining ingredients. Marinate at least 5 hours, or overnight. Split skin of turkey and rub sauce under it on meat, but do not remove skin. Grill turkey over charcoal coals, turning pieces frequently, and painting pieces with pastry brush dipped in melted butter. Cooking time, approximately 45 minutes.

BROILED TURKEY

Split a 5 or 6 pound young turkey down the back and remove breast bone so it can flatten out like a thick steak. Have at hand a bowl of melted butter, mixed with a little chopped garlic and parsley. Broil the turkey like a steak over a deep bed of coals. Baste liberally with the melted butter. Keep a bowl of water at hand. When flames spring up, sprinkle water (don't splash) on flames. By sprinkling lightly you create little steam clouds. After 45 minutes of this alternate steaming and broiling with frequent turnings you will have a broiled fowl that tastes the way pheasant is supposed to taste, and often doesn't.

WILD DUCKS—GRILLED

Clean the ducks, wipe well, and split down the back. Season with salt and pepper, rub with fine olive oil and place on the grill. Let them cook from 7 to 10 minutes on each side, turning them over at least twice. A wild duck is never cooked dry. It must just reach the point where the blood will not run if the flesh is pierced with fork in carving.

Place on a very hot dish and pour over them melted butter which has been mixed with lemon juice and minced parsley. Garnish with watercress or parsley sprigs.

PHEASANT

Halve or quarter the bird, then marinate pieces in a mixture of half olive oil and half white wine. Sprinkle drained sections with paprika just before cooking. Broil on the grill, basting often with the oil-wine mixture. Add a little sprinkle of salt before serving. The oil-wine blend is used for basting because it does not dominate the natural flavor of the pheasant. Serves 6.

QUAIL

Clean and wipe the birds well. Cut them through the back and spread. Rub them with melted butter and season with salt and freshly ground pepper to taste. Fasten a strip of bacon to breast of each bird with skewers. Place on the grill and cook for 15 or 20 minutes, according to size. Cook breast side up. Serve on buttered toast, allowing a slice for each bird.

SQUAB

Brush whole squabs inside and out with soy sauce; barbecue 20 to 25 minutes, turning and basting occasionally with mixture of soy sauce and melted butter.

FISH

MACKEREL

Clean, cut off the head, and dry with a damp cloth; do not wash. Split open and flatten out. Soak in a solution of salt and water (plenty of salt) for 24 hours. Then wash off all traces of salt and paint liberally with liquid smoke. Grill lightly for 5 minutes to a side over oak bark coals. Serve hot or cold. Makes a good snack, or even a meal with salad and beer.

TROUT

Trout, when wrapped in bacon, fastened with a skewer, and cooked on the barbecue grill is a dish fit for the gods. Cook over glowing coals in a hinged, double rack, and by the time the bacon is cooked crisp, the fish is done also.

PRAWNS

1 pound raw (green) prawns
½ cup dark molasses
1 can (8 oz.) Spanish style tomato sauce
½ teaspoon salt
½ teaspoon freshly ground pepper
1 teaspoon dry mustard
¼ teaspoon Tabasco
Pinch of thyme
¼ cup salad or olive oil

Wash, shuck, and clean raw prawns. Toss into boiling salted water, reduce heat, and simmer for 15 minutes. Drain and cool, but do not rinse as this tends to toughen them. Mix all the rest of the ingredients together to make the sauce. If you do not like too hot a mixture, cut down on the pepper, mustard, and Tabasco. Add the cooked prawns and turn in the sauce until completely covered. Scoop out the prawns and arrange on the barbecue grill or thread on skewers. Cook over hot coals. Turn prawns two or three times and baste frequently with the sauce left in the bowl. Serve hot, right from the grill. This is finger food, so have plenty of napkins near by. This amount will serve 4 when used as appetizers. Double the recipe, if serving them as a main dish.

Pickled prawns make good appetizers served as is or with a sauce. Simmer them in a mixture of half wine vinegar and half water that has been seasoned with pickling spices, curry powder, onion, and a couple of cloves of garlic. These should not be drained but should chill right in the pickling liquid.

TABANGAS BAKED FISH

Select a good 5 to 7-pound salmon, striped bass, or steelhead. Clean, leaving head and tail intact. Stuff with this dressing:

2 cups chopped tomatoes
½ cup chopped onions
1 teaspoon ginger
1 teaspoon salt
Soy sauce to taste
Lemon juice to taste
Dash of Tabasco
Little minced garlic

Fasten edges of fish together with skewers or toothpicks, and wrap whole fish in greased butcher paper or a large sweet leaf, such as banana. Bake over charcoal fire for about 2 hours. Serves 6 to 8.

OYSTERS IN BACON WRAP

Season oysters with salt and pepper, and wrap each oyster in a thin strip of bacon and secure the wrapping with wooden toothpicks. Arrange the "blanketed" oysters in a hinged, double, wire rack. Barbecue quickly over a hot bed of coals, turning often. As soon as the bacon has "sizzled" to your fancy, your barbecued oysters are done.

Serve with sliced lemon, a little drawn butter, A-1 sauce and Tabasco, not forgetting, of course, a cold bottle of Sauterne or Hock, the natural accompaniment of oysters.

GRILLED SALMON

Clean fish and remove heads. Flatten out in a triangular shape by completely splitting the fish through the tail and pressing them. Layer them in rock salt overnight. Rinse well with cold water and dry; place in hinged wire grill frame or in rack improvised from chicken wire. Broil flesh side down for 1½ hours, then expose other side. Total cooking time about 2½ to 3 hours. For fuel, use alderwood, damp and green, to assure plenty of smoke.

GRILLED SALMON

Variation: Fill body cavity of cleaned salmon with chopped onions, parsley, and salt; place fish on square of chicken wire, fold over and hook loose ends, and place on grill. When cooked, the skin will adhere to the chicken wire, which is discarded.

BROILED SALMON

An application of lemon juice adds greatly to the flavor of broiled or pan-fried salmon steaks. About an hour before cooking, brush both sides of each steak with lemon juice, cover loosely with waxed paper, and place in the refrigerator. When ready to cook, dust with flour, salt, and pepper. Then pan-fry in heated butter or place on the grill.

BASS AND SAUSAGE

For a novelty, stuff bass with Mexican sausage, and grill over the coals. Type of sausage used is known as "chorizo."

LOBSTER

Kill lobster by inserting knife in back between body and tail shells. Split lengthwise and clean. Wash and dry carefully. Brush

meat with melted butter or oil. Dust with salt and pepper. Broil (shell side down) until shell browns. Turn over and brown meaty side. Baste frequently with butter or oil. Serve with melted butter and lemon juice.

FRUIT & VEGETABLES

GRILLED FRUITS

Little need be done to fruits for grilling. Bananas, slightly under-ripe, will grill in their skins in about 8 minutes. Wedges of fresh pineapple will grill to a beautiful golden brown with nothing added to them. Drained canned pineapple or peach halves can be treated the same way, or they can be brushed with melted butter and lightly dredged with brown sugar before grilling.

FRESH PINEAPPLE

Cut a fresh pineapple of average size lengthwise into 8 sections. Place in baking pan and drip honey—about a tablespoon to a section—over the fruit. Let stand for ½ hour and then grill over an open fire.

HONEY-GRILLED BANANAS

Do not peel the bananas. Make a slit about 3 inches long in the skin. Force 1 tablespoon of honey into this opening and let stand for ½ hour. Place on grill and cook for about 8 minutes, turning frequently.

BROILED GRAPEFRUIT

Cut grapefruit in halves and remove seeds. Loosen segments from the skin and section membranes. Cover with brown or white sugar to start the juice running, and after half an hour, add more sugar, if desired. Dot the tops with butter, pour about a tablespoon of Sherry or Rum over each half Place on grill and broil until fruit is thoroughly heated and slightly browned on top.

GRILLED VEGETABLES

Tomatoes cut in half, eggplant cut in ¼-inch slices, zucchini cut in wedges—all can be brushed with seasoned oil and then grilled. If the bars on your grill are too far apart, put the vegetables in a double hinged wire broiler. Allow 10 or 15 minutes for cooking.

GRILLED EARS OF CORN

Strip the ears down to the last 3 or 4 husks and place in ice water 30 minutes or longer. Drain well and place on the grill for only 15 or 20 minutes. Delicious with lots of melted butter and salt!

Variation: Dip the ears in heavily salted water, lay them right on top of the coals, and cook 8 to 10 minutes, turning frequently to prevent burning.

ROASTED CORN ON THE COB

Use only unhusked ears. Lay back husks and remove silk. Return husks to their former position and wire into place (with any fine wire) at center and near the tip of cob, covering the kernels as well as possible. Roast on the grill, turning 3 or 4 times so that all surfaces are exposed to the heat. Snip the wires with wire cutter, husk the ears (gloves are necessary) and serve.

Variation: Open the husk at one end and let about 2 tablespoons of barbecue sauce run inside the ear. Smooth husk back in place; tie and cook as above.

BAKED POTATOES

If you have no built-in oven, and dislike baking potatoes in ashes, use an inexpensive sheet-iron oven designed for use over a gas burner. Set it over a corner of the grill and the potatoes will be baked beautifully without charred skins.

Another way to bake potatoes is to place the scrubbed potatoes, rubbed well with bacon drippings or butter, on a wire rack which holds them up about 3/8 of an inch above a flat plate. Then cover them with a roaster lid. Baked this way, they must be turned and moved frequently, to prevent over-charring of the skin. To serve, wipe the skins with a clean cloth, slightly mash the ends toward the middle, cut open and put butter in the hole. Butter which has been softened, mixed with chopped chives and then chilled firm again, is especially good in barbecue-baked potatoes.

GRILLED FRENCH BREAD

Cut sour French bread in half lengthwise and toast over the hot embers. Melt butter in shallow pan and dip the toasted bread into it.

Variation for garlic eaters: Mince garlic and work into soft butter—spread on toasted French bread.

ROASTING ON THE SPIT

ROAST SUCKLING PIG

Ask your butcher to provide you with a cleaned, tender suckling pig about 30 pounds in weight. A young pig any smaller will be nothing but skin and bones when cooked.

Stuff with a sage or fruit dressing. Don't stuff it in too tightly, as the dressing will expand. Sew it in with heavy string and lace it closely and tightly.

Leave the skin on. Head and feet can be cut off either before or after cooking; it is easier done before—but it won't look much like a pig. Insert a piece of wood in the mouth to simplify adding an apple later. Truss the legs with cord in a kneeling position, and place pig on spit over a deep bed of hot coals. Coals should be arranged in such a way to allow for a pan to be placed in the center to catch the drippings from the roasting meat, which should be used for basting. The pig can be basted with oil, but it will lose some of its flavor. Cooking time: 6 to 10 hours, depending on the fire.

When done, remove from the spit, place a red apple in the mouth, cranberries or cherries in the eye sockets, and place it on a bed

of watercress. Various garnishes of vegetable flowers, radish roses, stuffed stewed apricots and prunes, or holly berries, may be added.

Bring the roast pig to the table with the head separated from the body, the cut ringed with a wreath of watercress and flowers. In carving, first separate the shoulder from the carcass, and remove the legs. This will leave the ribs open to the knife. Cut down the back bone, remove the loins and serve the tender chops from sliced loins.

BARBECUED HAM

Make your fire of prune or fruit wood, approximately two or three inches in diameter, and enough charcoal to keep the bed of coals at an even heat. Lay a 7-pound shank of tenderized ham directly on the grill for about 15 minutes on each side. Then take it off the fire and remove the skin. Leave fat on and score. Now spit, or skewer, the ham and cook it from 3½ to 4 hours, basting it as it cooks. The outside fat will char black, but don't let that worry you. Just don't let it burn. Keep the fire constant. When ham is done, break off charred fat with a knife. Put back on spit for another 10 or 15 minutes and use up remainder of basting sauce. Remove ham, cut off excess fat, slice, and serve. Serves 6 to 8.

Baste with this sauce:

1 tablespoon cinnamon
1 tablespoon dry mustard
1 tablespoon ginger
½ tablespoon whole cloves
1½ to 2 ounces whisky or gin
2 tablespoons brown sugar
½ tablespoon molasses
⅔ cup wine vinegar
Pineapple juice

Place the cinnamon, mustard, ginger, and cloves in a mortar, or small jar, and cover with the whiskey or gin. (The alcohol will dissolve the essential oils, and that's what gives the flavor.) Let set for an hour or so. Put the brown sugar, molasses, and vinegar in a pint jar. Grind the spices with a pestle, or stir well, and add to the vinegar-sugar solution. Pour in enough pineapple juice to make a pint. Stir well. Now you are ready to paint your ham. Mix the sauce each time you baste, so that the spices are evenly distributed. Don't leave any dregs in the jar, put them all on the ham to get the full, spicy flavor.

LEG OF PORK

A leg of pork may be barbecued on the spit (or grill)—providing you keep a bed of coals going for 8 to 9 hours.

Place a 14 to 16-pound leg on the spit, shield it if possible to keep in all the heat, and roast for 6 or 7 hours before basting. Cook for about 2 hours longer, basting frequently with Southern Barbecue Sauce, recipe on page 44.

When served, it should be sliced with the grain, parallel to the bone, not across the grain.

BARBECUED BOLOGNA ROLL

Remove casing from large round bologna. Score top surface as you do for ham. Insert skewer down center or place on spit. Grill over coals, basting frequently with barbecue sauce.

ROLLED RIB OF BEEF

This is excellent for serving a crowd; it is easy to slice in convenient serving-size pieces. Have the butcher roll a rib of beef. Make several small incisions in the surface of roast and insert small pieces of peeled onion and fresh thyme. Rub surface of roast lightly with smoked salt. Place on spit and grill, basting frequently with barbecue sauce. When done slice in rounds and serve on buttered rolls.

LAMB SHOULDER

- 4 cloves garlic, minced
- 2 large onions, minced
- 1 green pepper, minced
- 2 tablespoons salt
- 1 tablespoon freshly ground pepper
- 2 cans (6 oz.) tomato paste
- 1 pint water
- Rosemary and thyme to taste
- Dried celery leaves to taste
- Dash of Tabasco
- 1 pint red wine
- 4 lamb shoulders

Simmer all ingredients except the wine for about 1 hour, stirring often. Remove from stove, cool, and stir in the red wine. Place about 1 pint of the sauce in a jar (saving the rest for later, of course) and take it to your favorite butcher. Have the butcher bone the lamb shoulders, cover the insides well with the contents of your jar, and then roll them as any rolled roast.

Bring the rolled roast home, spit it over a good bed of coals, and baste frequently with the remainder of the sauce. Cooking time 1½ to 2 hours. Serves 24 (6 to each lamb shoulder).

LEG OF LAMB

Wipe leg of lamb with a damp cloth. Sprinkle with salt, pepper, and a little flour. Rub into meat. Slash and insert cut pieces of garlic. Place on spit and baste frequently with this sauce:

- 3 tablespoons Worcestershire sauce
- 3 tablespoons meat sauce
- ½ cup tomato catsup
- 2 tablespoons butter or margarine
- 3 tablespoons shortening
- 1 tablespoon sugar
- 1 tablespoon vinegar
- 2 teaspoons liquid smoke
- 1 medium-sized onion, grated
- 1 teaspoon salt
- Few drops Tabasco sauce

Combine ingredients in a small saucepan and heat to boiling.

ROAST TURKEY

Remove bird from refrigerator 2 or 3 hours before cooking. Loosen neck skin and cut off neck close to the body, leaving the flap of skin. Put neck, heart, and gizzard to cook in about 1½ quarts of water with several sprigs of parsley and celery tops, and a sliced onion; simmer until very tender, then drop in the liver and cook 15 minutes longer. Set aside to use in making stuffing and/or gravy. Rub inside of bird with salt and pepper, then stuff with dressing.

Stitch or skewer the flap of neck-skin to back of bird, and sew up or skewer-and-lace the body opening. Truss bird into compact shape, and slide on spit. Test it for balance, then lock in place with locking tines. Rub it all over with melted turkey fat or oil, and place bird in position over coals. As it cooks, baste with sauce (page 47).

Clear an oval in the coals and place a pan in center of the ring of coals to catch drippings from the roasting bird. Scoop out drippings with a long-handled spoon and add to basting sauce. Cooking time: 10-13 pounds, 20 minutes per pound, 14-17 pounds, 15-18 minutes per pound; 18-25 pounds, 12-15 minutes per pound.

BREAD STUFFING

Allow about 1 cup bread crumbs for each pound dressed weight.

- 3 quarts soft white bread crumbs
- 1 to 2 teaspoons rubbed sage, thyme, OR marjoram (or all three)
- 2 to 3 teaspoons salt
- ½ teaspoon black pepper
- 2 medium-sized onions
- 1 cup celery tops, finely chopped
- ¾ to 1 cup melted butter or margarine
- 1 cup broth from cooked giblets

SKEWER COOKING

LAMB EN BROCHETTE

- 4 tablespoons olive oil
- 6 tablespoons soy sauce
- 1/4 teaspoon freshly ground pepper
- 1 large onion, grated fine
- 3 tablespoons lemon juice
- 3 to 4 pounds lean lamb meat

Mix ingredients together to make a marinade. Cut lamb into cubes and leave in the marinade for an hour or longer, turning and rubbing the seasonings into the meat. Thread on skewers and broil. Serves 6.

MARINATED LAMB

- 5 pound leg of lamb
- 1/2 pound onions, peeled, sliced
- 1 tablespoon salt
- 1/2 teaspoon pepper
- 1/2 cup Sherry
- 2 tablespoons olive oil
- 1 teaspoon oregano

Night before the barbecue, trim fat and gristle from the leg of lamb and cut lean meat into 2-inch cubes. Put in a large bowl and mix with a sauce made of the ingredients above. Leave in marinade overnight. Put 4 to 6 cubes of meat on skewers and grill for 15 to 20 minutes or longer. Serves 4.

LAMB COMBINATIONS

String skewers with lamb cubes, alternating with small, ripe, unpeeled tomatoes and small peeled onions; or squares of bacon and mushrooms; or cubes of parboiled eggplant (brushed with oil) and wedges of tomatoes.

LAMB IN ONION JUICE

- 2 pounds lean lamb
- 2 medium-sized onions
- ½ cup salad oil
- 1 bay leaf
- 1 teaspoon salt
- ½ teaspoon thyme
- Pinch of sage
- 3 peppercorns, crushed
- 1 cup Sherry (or red wine)

Cut the lamb into cubes about an inch square and put them in an earthen bowl. Run the two onions through the food grinder, using the finest blade. Place the onion pulp in a small muslin sack or a cloth and squeeze the juice onto the meat. Add the oil, bay leaf, and seasonings, working them into the meat. Add the wine and let everything stand—at least overnight. Then spike the meat on skewers and broil to your taste. You can alternate pieces of bacon, onion, green peppers, or even very small tomatoes with the lamb.

SHISH KEBAB

Buy 1 pound of leg of lamb per person, plus 2 or 3 extra pounds. Lamb shoulder may be used, too. Plan on 1⅓ "shish" (skewer load) per person.

- 1 medium-sized onion per person
- 1 package or jar dried oregano (you won't use all of it)
- Salt
- Cayenne
- Italian red pepper
- Black pepper
- ½ cup wine, wine vinegar, or vinegar
- 2 tablespoons olive oil
- 1 medium-sized green pepper per "shish"
- 1½ medium-sized tomatoes per "shish"

A day ahead of time prepare the meat as follows: Cut the boned leg of lamb into steaks, crosswise down the length of the leg, about 1¼ inches to 1½ inches thick; then into cubes. Cut out any gristle. A small strip of fat may be left on the cubes if desired. Place meat in a bowl and salt to taste. Pepper with the three different kinds of pepper, but not too much for it will kill the flavor of the meat. Add about 1 rounded tablespoon of oregano for each leg of lamb. Cut onions into thin strips and place in the bowl with the meat. Pour over all the wine or vinegar and olive oil. Mix well and allow this to marinate in your refrigerator overnight.

Save the lamb bones and leftovers to make the broth used in preparing "pilaff," an accompanying rice dish, the recipe for which is given on page 62.

Cut the tomatoes into chunks about the same size as the meat. Do not skin. Small Italian pear-shaped tomatoes are good used whole. Cut the peppers into pieces big enough to bend and be skewered. Beginning with a piece of meat, then tomato, and pepper, skewer three of each alternately on each "shish." Broil for 15 to 20 minutes over a good bed of coals.

Heat the marinade, add chopped tomatoes to suit taste, and use for sauce.

LAMB AND HAM SHISH KEBAB

Using about 7 pounds of shoulder or leg of lamb for 7-8 people, cut the lamb in cubes.

Soak 6-8 hours in Claret—enough nearly to cover meat; add slices of onion and garlic to your taste.

Place on skewers, alternating the lamb with small pieces of tenderized ham. Season with salt and pepper. Broil over charcoal fire.

SKEWERED MINTED LAMB

Marinade and basting sauce:

- ½ ounce dry mint leaves
- 1 teaspoon dry tarragon leaves
- ½ cup vinegar
- ¾ cup brown sugar
- 1 teaspoon dry mustard
- ½ teaspoon salt
- ½ cup butter
- Juice of ½ lemon and grated peel
- ½ cup Sauterne

Put all ingredients except Sauterne into a saucepan and bring to a boil. Remove from heat, cover pan, and let steep for about 30 minutes. Strain, and add Sauterne. Cool. Marinate meat in this sauce for 30 minutes.

For each serving, use:

- 3 pieces lean lamb, cut in squares
- 2 small green tomatoes
- 2 slices onion, cut ½ inch thick
- 6 squares sliced bacon

Alternate the above items on skewers. Broil, basting frequently with sauce until done. Serve with rice, sour French bread, and tossed green salad.

CHINESE SHISH KEBAB

Dip cubes of lamb or pork in a mixture of soy sauce, cornstarch, and peanut oil. If available, add fresh ginger root, mashed. Skewer between slices of green pepper and cook over coals. Serve with sauce made from 1 part prepared mustard to 3 parts catsup.

LAMB OR BEEF KEBABS

- 1½ pounds meat (use either beef round or lamb shoulder) cut in 1-inch cubes
- ½ cup tomato catsup
- 1 teaspoon salt
- 2 tablespoons sugar
- 2 tablespoons beefsteak sauce
- 2 tablespons cider vinegar
- 2 tablespoons Worcestershire sauce
- ¼ cup water
- 2 tablespoons salad oil or shortening

Place cubed meat in bowl; combine remaining ingredients in saucepan and heat to boiling. Pour over meat; let stand several hours or overnight in marinade. String on skewers and broil over hot coals. Re-heat marinating liquid for sauce. Serves 4.

LAMB LIVER

- 1 whole lamb liver
- 5 medium-sized onions
- 4 cloves garlic, mashed
- Salt and allspice to taste
- 1 large bunch celery

Buy the freshest lamb liver you can get, and cut it into 1-inch cubes, and place in bowl. Add onions, cut in 4 parts lengthwise (do not cut the bottom stem, just peel outside skin, otherwise the onion sections will fall apart). Add the mashed garlic and seasonings. Chop the bunch of celery, including the leaves, and place in bowl. Mix all ingredients together and set in refrigerator for 2 hours.

Place on skewers, alternating an onion quarter with 3 or 4 cubes of liver. Use remaining vegetables for salad.

SKEWERED STEAK AND MUSHROOMS

Well-marinated squares of tender beef, and fresh mushrooms, threaded on skewers and broiled, make good outdoor eating.

- ½ cup Burgundy or claret wine
- 1 teaspoon Worcestershire sauce
- 1 clove garlic
- ½ cup salad oil
- 2 tablespoons catsup
- 1 teaspoon sugar
- ½ teaspoon salt
- ½ teaspoon monosodium glutamate
- 1 tablespoon vinegar
- ½ teaspoon marjoram
- ½ teaspoon rosemary
- 1 pound sirloin steak
- 12 large fresh mushrooms

Mix wine with Worcestershire sauce, peeled garlic clove, salad oil, catsup, and seasonings. Cut meat into 2-inch squares. Wash mushrooms thoroughly. Marinate steak squares and mushrooms in wine mixture for 2 hours. Alternate meat squares and mushrooms on skewers. Broil, turning on all sides, basting frequently with remaining marinade. Serves 4.

FRANKFURTERS

Cut franks in 1-inch lengths, spread with prepared mustard, and string on skewers alternately with thick slices of dill pickle and onion wedges.

Or, split lengthwise, insert a strip of cheese, wrap with bacon strip secured at both ends with toothpicks, and place on skewer

GROUND BEEF

- 1 pound ground meat
- 2 eggs
- ½ cup dry bread crumbs
- 1 tablespoon prepared mustard
- ½ teaspoon salt

Combine ground meat with eggs (beaten), bread crumbs, mustard, and salt. Divide into 6 or 8 parts and squeeze each portion of meat around the skewer. Serves 6 to 8.

Variation: Use the above combination of ground beef and form into 6 or 8 thick patties; encircle each with a strip of bacon and let stand for several hours. Skewer patties crosswise.

SKEWERED HAMBURGER

- Garlic, finely chopped
- Salt and pepper
- ½ cup olive oil
- 1 pound ground beef
- ½ cup finely chopped onion

Put finely chopped garlic, salt, and pepper into olive oil and stir thoroughly. Place hamburger in large bowl and cover with onion. Add olive oil mixture, and combine. Knead with hands to mix onions thoroughly through meat and to permit complete absorption of oil. Take barbecue skewers and form meat around skewers to about 1½-inch in diameter. Length of meat along skewer may be varied to suit size of buns into which it will be placed. Barbecue over charcoal, turning continuously to keep juices in and upon meat. Skin meat off skewers into buns and serve directly to customers. Have mustard and catsup ready in case it's needed. Serves 6.

HAMBURGERS EN BROCHETTE

Form seasoned meat loaf mixture in balls the size of a small egg. String 2 or 3 meat balls on skewers, alternating with onion and quarters of unpeeled tomato. Sprinkle with salt or brush with barbecue sauce. Grill until done.

Alternate: Mold seasoned meat around skewer, and wrap with a slice of bacon. Dip in sauce when done.

BEEF COMBINATIONS

String skewers with cubes of beef with dividers of: onion quarters and tomato wedges; squares of pre-cooked pork, dipped in beaten egg and crumbs and brushed with oil or shortening; or squares of ham and pineapple wedges.

STEAK KEBABS

Secure bay tree sticks from the hills. (Any green sticks may be used but the bay sticks add aroma and flavor.) Wash and whittle them to a point at the smaller end. Pieces of steak cut about 3 or 4 inches square are spiked on the stick, leaving about an inch or so between each 2 pieces. This, of course, is to allow the meat to cook on all sides. Salt and pepper the meat and then hold or prop your stick over the fire until the meat is done to your own liking. It usually takes 20 to 30 minutes. Top round steak from good beef may be used for this.

ROLLED STEAK

Slice sirloin tip across the grain with a very sharp knife, making thin slices about the size of the palm of the hand. Cut fat bacon lengthwise into narrow strips about ⅛-inch wide. Put a strip inside the slice of beef and roll up; pin with toothpicks. Slide roll on skewer and broil.

CAMP KEBABS

Apples
White onions, medium-sized
Beef or lamb
Bacon

Cut cored apples into ½-inch thick rings. Slice onions into ¼-inch slices. Allow 2 slices of each of these, 2 1-inch cubes of beef or lamb, a long strip of bacon, and a pointed stick for each kebab. (The stick should be freshly cut from a willow so that it will be too green to burn while the food is cooking.)

Run the point of the stick through one end of the slice of bacon, top with a ring of apple, then the onion slice, and next a cube of meat. Lap the bacon up over this and run the stick through it again. Repeat the layers of apple, onion and meat and draw the other end of the bacon up over this and secure on the end of the stick. Hold over glowing coals until the bacon is very crisp and the meat is done—about 20 minutes.

LIVER

Skewer calves-liver cubes with bacon and whole mushrooms. For chicken liver, alternate with small bacon squares.

PARBOILED SAUSAGE

Parboil sausage briefly and string with slices or cubes of unpeeled apple.

FOIL KEBABS

To cook kebabs in foil: Thread meat, onion, green pepper, and tomato cubes on a skewer or a thin stick. Wrap in a double thickness of foil, place on coals, and cook for about 14 minutes.

VEAL SATI

2 pounds veal steak, cut in 1-inch squares
¼ cup soy sauce
Juice of 1 lemon
2 tablespoons oil

Run each skewer through the center of 4 to 6 meat squares. Mix the rest of the ingredients and pour over the skewered meat. Let stand 3 or 4 hours. Broil over glowing coals 15 to 20 minutes, or till a golden brown. Turn as necessary to cook evenly and baste with the sauce once during the broiling. Serves 4 to 6.

SKEWERED CHICKEN LIVERS

18 chicken livers
6 slices bacon
Salt and pepper
Mushrooms
Olive oil
Bread crumbs
Butter, melted
Lemon juice
Parsley

Cut away gall from chicken livers, and dry well with clean cloth. Season with pinch of salt and pepper. Cut livers in half. Broil bacon slices, one minute to each side, and cut each slice into 6 pieces. Take 6 skewers, run one through center of liver slice, then a mushroom, then a piece of bacon, and repeat until all skewers are filled. Roll in olive oil, dip in fresh bread crumbs, and broil over coals. Arrange on a hot dish, and over them pour melted butter to which lemon juice and chopped parsley have been added. Serves 6.

CHICKEN LIVERS WITH WATER CHESTNUTS

Use fresh (wash thoroughly) or canned water chestnuts; slice into 3 parts. Slice chicken livers and dip in soy sauce; place slice of water chestnut between two slices of chicken liver, wrap in thin strip of bacon, place on skewer, and broil.

VEGETABLES

Potatoes, sweet potatoes, summer squash, and eggplant are easily cooked on skewers. Parboil in salted water until not quite done and still firm enough to hold together well. Thread on skewers, brush with oil, and broil.

BONFIRE "BIG APPLES"

Caramel apples make a wonderful dessert and a fitting finish to a barbecue supper. Oldsters as well as youngsters enjoy making them and eating them, too.

Let each person prepare a long, selected stick by slightly charring the sharpened end in the fire and then plunging it immediately into cold water.

Impale a nice plump apple on the end of the stick, through the stem end.

Roast the apple over the coals until the skin may be easily peeled off. Tear off the peel, and roll the hot apple in a pan of brown sugar. Return the sugared apple to the fire and turn it slowly while the sugar melts into candy. You'll know what to do next.

CAMPFIRE OYSTERS

Use skewers, or cut long green sticks, peel and sharpen ends. Cut thin strips of bacon into fourths. Alternate on the stick with drained oysters, ending and beginning with a piece of bacon. Three large oysters and four pieces of bacon are sufficient for one sandwich. Cook until bacon is well broiled and edges of oysters curl. Push off onto bread or bun. Season with salt and pepper and squeeze a little lemon juice over oysters.

FISH

Cut marinated fish fillets into small cubes or slices, skewer with a wedge of tomato and a tiny piece of bayleaf between each portion.

SHRIMP

Skewer whole large shrimp or prawns with dividers of pineapple wedges and bacon.

Variation: Peel large shrimps. Dip in soy sauce, drain, skewer, and broil over coals.

SAUCES & MARINADES

STEAK SAUCE

- 1 bunch green onions
- 3 cloves garlic, minced
- Butter for sautéing
- 1 cup catsup
- ½ cup wine vinegar
- 1 teaspoon Worcestershire sauce
- ½ teaspoon EACH of celery salt, garlic salt, onion salt, chili powder, dry mustard, and dried mixed herbs

Cut up green onions and garlic in small pieces and sauté in butter until brown. Mix remaining ingredients in a bowl, then add the sautéed onions and garlic. Marinate steaks in this mixture for 3 hours before grilling.

BARNEY'S BARBECUE SAUCE

- ¼ cup vinegar
- ¼ cup catsup
- ½ cup Worcestershire sauce
- ¾ cup water
- 1½ teaspoons dry mustard
- ¾ teaspoon salt
- ¼ cube butter, melted
- ¼ cup chopped onion
- ½ teaspoon sugar
- ¼ teaspoon chili powder
- Small clove garlic
- Dash of red pepper

This sauce is good with spareribs, venison, or may be served over steamed wild rice. May be used as either marinade or basting sauce.

SMOKY SAUCE

Add 1 tablespoon or more of liquid smoke, according to strength desired, to about 1 pint of your favorite barbecue sauce. Let meat or shish kebab stand in sauce for several hours or overnight to absorb flavors; use as basting sauce while the meat is barbecuing.

THICK SAUCE

- 2 tablespoons lard or shortening
- 2 tablespoons flour
- 4 small cans (8 oz.) tomato sauce
- 1 tablespoon Worcestershire sauce
- 5 tablespoons chili powder
- Few drops Tabasco sauce
- 2 cloves (or powdered equivalent)

Heat fat until very hot. Add flour and stir until slightly browned. Add the rest of the ingredients and cook until thick. If too thick, add a little water, but it should not be a thin sauce.

CIRCLE J SAUCE

- 1 clove garlic, minced
- 1 small onion, minced
- ¾ teaspoon dry mustard
- 1 tablespoon grated fresh horseradish
- 1 tablespoon mixed minced herbs (thyme, marjoram, parsley)
- 2 tablespoons vinegar
- 3 cups water
- 1 tablespoon A-1 or Worcestershire sauce
- ⅔ cup butter
- ½ cup catsup
- ½ teaspoon juice from a bottle of Tabasco peppers
- 2 teaspoons sugar
- ¾ teaspoon chili powder
- ¼ teaspoon black pepper, freshly ground
- ¾ teaspoon salt

Combine all ingredients and cook slowly for 45 minutes. Use to baste meat or fish while cooking, or dip slices or chunks of hot cooked meat into the heated sauce before serving.

ALKI POINT SAUCE

- 2 tablespoons finely minced onion
- 3 tablespoons finely minced green pepper
- 1 tablespoon butter
- ½ cup water
- 1 medium-sized tomato, diced
- ½ teaspoon salt
- ⅛ teaspoon pepper
- ¼ teaspoon Kitchen Bouquet
- Dash of celery salt

Sauté onion and green pepper in the butter until they are golden brown. Add water, tomatoes, and seasonings. Bring to a boil. Simmer for 10 minutes, stirring frequently. Makes enough sauce for four meat servings.

MARINADE

1 cup Zinfandel
1 cup olive oil
2 or 3 cloves garlic
1 bay leaf
2 or 3 sprigs rosemary
2 or 3 sprigs thyme
2 or 3 sprigs marjoram

Mix all together and set away in refrigerator. This preparation will keep indefinitely and will do for several barbecue occasions. The herbs may be strained out after the mixture is well flavored. Cover steaks with the sauce and let stand in a covered dish for from 6 to 36 hours before barbecuing. The sauce may also be used for basting when the meat is on the grill. Apply with a long stalk of celery, using the leaves on the end as a swab. The celery also gives a flavor.

BASIC BEEF SAUCE

2 cups tomato juice
1 teaspoon mustard
1 tablespoon sugar
3 tablespoons vinegar
2 teaspoons horseradish
1 tablespoon Worcestershire sauce
¼ cup grated onion
1 clove garlic, minced
¼ cup catsup
½ cup butter or margarine
Few drops of Tabasco sauce
¾ teaspoon salt
½ teaspoon paprika
½ teaspoon freshly ground pepper

Simmer all ingredients for 30 minutes. For a different flavor, substitute meat stock for the tomato juice, or use half and half.

SAUCE JEREZ

¼ pound process Cheddar cheese
½ cup Sherry
1 teaspoon dry mustard
½ teaspoon seasoning salt
¼ teaspoon paprika
Salt to taste

Melt cheese in double boiler and add wine, a little at a time, stirring constantly. When well blended, add seasonings, stirring thoroughly. Serve hot over steaks, lamb chops or other meat dishes.

RAW TOMATO RELISH

1 green chili pepper
1 large or 2 small tomatoes
1 small white onion
Salt

Place the green chili pepper on a fork and hold it over open flame until it is seared and the skin is broken. Then wrap in a dry towel for a few minutes to steam. Remove stem and skin, split, and remove ALL seeds (they contain most of the heat). Grind the pepper together with the tomato; add the onion. Serve at room temperature with beef, lamb, mutton, or fish. Serves 2-4.

QUENTIN BARBECUE SAUCE

- 1 good-sized onion, finely chopped
- 3 or 4 cloves garlic, minced
- 1 sprig parsley, minced
- 2 cups catsup
- ½ cup wine vinegar
- 1 cup olive oil
- 2 tablespoons Worcestershire sauce
- Freshly ground pepper to taste

Put ingredients in order given into a quart jar, cover and shake so ingredients will be well blended. Let stand 24 hours, shaking occasionally during the day.

GARLIC SAUCE

- 1 clove garlic, minced
- ½ cup salad oil, olive oil or melted butter

Put the garlic to soak in oil the night before the barbecue. Or, if butter is used, melt and keep warm, with the clove of garlic floating in it about 2 hours before the meat is to be grilled. Use for basting grilled steaks or chops.

EASY-TO-MAKE SAUCE

- 1 can (8 oz.) tomato sauce
- 4 teaspoons Worcestershire sauce
- ¼ teaspoon each celery, onion, and garlic salt
- 4 tablespoons Sherry
- 1 tablespoon wine vinegar
- 2 tablespoons olive oil
- 1 clove garlic, minced

Combine all ingredients. Place in a covered jar and let stand in refrigerator overnight, or at least for several hours.

SANDWICH SAUCE

This sauce is not for basting, but is served over barbecued meats and in sandwiches.

- 1 clove of garlic, minced
- 1 whole onion, minced
- 2 tablespoons oil
- 2 teaspoons chili powder
- 1 teaspoon dry mustard
- 2 bay leaves
- ¼ teaspoon marjoram
- 1 can (No. 2½) tomatoes with puree, sieved
- ¼ cup vinegar
- ½ teaspoon celery salt

Cook the garlic and onion in oil about 5 minutes. Add the rest of the ingredients and simmer gently, stirring frequently, about 40 minutes or until mixture reaches desired thickness. Remove the bay leaves. It's ready for use or can be sealed in jars. If the sauce is heated before serving, the flavors of the meat and sauce are blended better.

SALSA (STEAK SANDWICH SAUCE)

- 4 onions, large
- 6 tomatoes
- 2 cans green chili, seeded
- Salt
- Freshly ground pepper
- 2 tablespoons wine vinegar
- ¼ cup olive oil

Mince onions, tomatoes, and green chili. Season with salt and pepper, add vinegar and olive oil. Let stand 2 hours before using.

PORTERHOUSE STEAK SAUCE

- ½ cup olive oil
- 3 tablespoons wine vinegar
- ½ tablespoon garlic salt
- 1 tablespoon paprika
- 1 teaspoon monosodium glutamate

Paint surfaces of steaks ½ hour before cooking; and again just before putting them on the fire. This amount is sufficient for 4 good-sized, porterhouse steaks.

SIMPLE STEAK SAUCE

- 1 cup olive oil
- 1 cup wine or wine vinegar
- 2 good-sized onions, grated or minced
- Garlic slices to suit taste
- 1 tablespoon salt
- 1 teaspoon freshly-ground pepper

Mix the oil and vinegar, then add the onion, garlic, salt and pepper. Pour into a pint fruit jar and stir until salt is dissolved. Let the mixture stand overnight, then stir well just before using.

ROASTING SAUCE

- ¼ pound butter
- 1 cup vinegar
- ½ teaspoon dry mustard
- 1 tablespoon chopped onions
- 2 tablespoons Worcestershire sauce
- 1 tablespoon chili sauce
- 1 teaspoon lemon juice
- 2 lemon slices
- 1 teaspoon brown sugar
- ½ pod red pepper, ground

Mix all ingredients together; put over low fire until the butter melts, then set where it will keep warm.

HAMBURGER SAUCE

For steaks or hamburgers. Enough for 6:

- 1 cube butter, melted
- ½ cup olive oil
- ½ cup catsup
- 1 teaspoon prepared mustard
- Dash of Worcestershire sauce
- Grated onion or garlic as desired
- Juice of ½ lemon
- Salt and freshly ground pepper

Shake well. Use either as a marinade or a basting sauce.

SAUCE FOR STEAKS OR CHOPS

½ cup peanut oil
¼ cup wine vinegar
1 or 2 tablespoons horseradish, freshly ground
1 cup hot water
2 tablespoons Worcestershire sauce
2 tablespoons grated onion juice and pulp
1 large clove garlic, grated or crushed
2 tablespoons chili sauce
1 tablespoon EACH of brown sugar, salt, dry mustard, paprika, black pepper
Generous sprigs EACH of fresh rosemary, fresh sage, fresh thyme, parsley

Simmer all ingredients together for about 15 minutes. Cool. Brush over patties while broiling; brush over both sides of chops or steak an hour before cooking. This sauce will keep satisfactorily for 2 weeks in the refrigerator.

WESTERN SAUCE

1 can (No. 2) tomatoes
2 cups water
1 can (6 oz.) tomato paste
2 dried chili peppers
½ cup tomato catsup
2 tablespoons sugar
2 teaspoons Worcestershire sauce
2 teaspoons chili powder
Juice 2 lemons
¼ cup wine vinegar
2½ teaspoons salt
¼ teaspoon cayenne
¼ teaspoon Tabasco
2 teaspoons freshly ground black pepper
1 large onion, chopped
1 clove garlic, chopped
2 bay leaves
½ pound butter
2 teaspoons dry mustard

Combine all ingredients and let simmer over low flame in covered pan for about 30 minutes. Strain through coarse sieve. This sauce can be kept several months in the refrigerator.

SOUTHERN BARBECUE SAUCE

1 quart cider vinegar
5 tablespoons Worcestershire sauce
2 tablespoons A-1 sauce
2 teaspoons salt
1 tablespoon sugar
6 whole mint leaves
¼ teaspoon paprika
4 shakes Tabasco
½ teaspoon black pepper
1½ tablespoons mixed whole pickling spices
1 bouillon cube
3 large slices unpeeled orange
2 large slices unpeeled lemon
1 cup water
1 tablespoon catsup
Sweet basil and oregano to taste

Put on the stove in an enamel or glass container, and simmer until the orange and lemon peel are pretty well cooked. Use this sauce on either pork or lamb. Excellent for basting spareribs.

BASIC PORK SAUCE

1½ cups tomato sauce
½ cup water
⅓ cup vinegar
⅓ cup brown sugar
2 tablespoons butter or margarine
1 teaspoon smoked salt
1 teaspoon ginger
½ teaspoon paprika
1 small onion, minced

Simmer all ingredients for 30 minutes.

VENISON SAUCE

Chop the following fresh herbs: 1 teaspoon each of marjoram, rosemary, sage, thyme. Add:

1 pint bottle of salad oil
⅔ pint wine vinegar
2 tablespoons Worcestershire sauce
⅓ cup parsley
Garlic (let your conscience be your guide, but plenty)

Mix thoroughly, adding salt and pepper to taste, and let the mixture stand overnight. Dip the venison chops or steaks in the sauce and cook, turning once or twice, until medium done.

BASIC LAMB SAUCE

¾ cup Sherry
1 slice lemon
1 sprig parsley, minced
2 tablespoons olive oil
1 teaspoon grated onion
1 teaspoon salt
½ teaspoon pepper
1 sprig each fresh rosemary and oregano, minced, or ½ teaspoon each dried herbs

Let stand for several hours to blend.

HERB SAUCE FOR LAMB

This recipe, using garden herbs for unusual flavor, was given to a "Sunset" reader by the great-grandson of one of the first Spanish governors of California.

1 small onion or half a large one
3 cloves garlic
2 sprigs rosemary
12 fresh mint leaves
¼ cup vinegar
½ cup water

Chop the onion and garlic fine and add the rosemary and mint leaves which have been crushed or chopped. Then add the vinegar and water and let the mixture stand overnight. When ready to barbecue steaks or chops, brush them thoroughly with the sauce, using a bunch of mint leaves for a brush. As the meat cooks, baste occasionally with more of the liquid. If still more sauce is desired, pass a cruet of it when serving. This is particularly fine for lamb.

KEBAB SAUCE

1 can (10½ oz.) condensed tomato soup
Oil or shortening
1 teaspoon dry mustard
1 teaspoon sugar (brown or granulated)
1 teaspoon salt
2 teaspoons chili powder
3 to 4 tablespoons wine or vinegar
Worcestershire sauce
Paprika
Pepper
1 onion, chopped fine
1 large clove garlic, chopped fine
Pinch rosemary leaves
1 tablespoon liquid smoke

Empty contents of can of tomato soup into a saucepan; fill can about three-fourths full of water, and add enough shortening or oil to bring water to top of the can; pour into saucepan. Add mustard, sugar, salt, chili powder, and wine or vinegar; Worcestershire sauce, paprika, and pepper to taste; chopped onion, chopped garlic, mashed well with a tiny bit of shortening; rosemary leaves, and liquid smoke. Heat to boiling and cook for about 5 minutes, or until all ingredients are well blended. Makes about 2¾ cups of sauce. May be made in quantity and stored in the refrigerator.

POULTRY MARINADE

This marinade will flavor 8 fryer halves (1¾ to 2½ pounds) or cut-up young turkeys.

2 to 3 cloves garlic
8 heaping teaspoons quick-cure salt (obtainable in rural localities)
1 level teaspoon EACH of thyme, celery salt, black pepper
2 heaping teaspoons dry mustard
½ teaspoon EACH of poultry seasoning, fresh grated ginger root, monosodium glutamate
¾ cup Sauterne
1 cup red wine vinegar
Olive oil

Mince garlic, put in bowl, add salt and crush together. Add other spices, then wine and vinegar. Do not add oil until ready to cook. Stir thoroughly until salt is dissolved, or shake well in covered jar. Put liquid in large bowl, dip each piece of fowl into it, place fowl in baking dish or flat pan, skin side down. Stir balance of marinade and pour over fowl. Let stand 2 to 3 hours, then turn fowl over and let stand again for 2 to 3 hours.

When ready to barbecue, pour marinade off fowl. Add olive oil to marinade in an amount equal to about ¼ the volume of marinade remaining. Stir thoroughly, brush each piece of fowl with mixture before placing on grill. Paint again each time fowl is turned.

A simplified version of this sauce is used to flavor steaks:

- 8 teaspoons quick-cure salt
- 1 teaspoon black pepper
- ¾ cup Sauterne
- 1 cup red wine vinegar
- ½ teaspoon monosodium glutamate
- Olive oil

Mix ingredients together, and soak steaks for 2 to 3 hours. Remove steaks from marinade, add olive oil ¼ by volume and baste steak while grilling.

COWBOY BARBECUE SAUCE

This sauce is sufficient for 8 to 10 chickens or the same amount, by weight, of meat.

- 2 cups butter or margarine
- 5 cups water
- ½ cup vinegar
- 2 teaspoons dry mustard
- 2 tablespoons sugar
- 1½ tablespoons each of salt, chili powder, and paprika
- ¼ teaspoon cayenne
- 1 tablespoon each Worcestershire sauce, Tabasco sauce, and black pepper
- 1 medium-sized onion, chopped fine
- 1 clove garlic, minced

Mix all ingredients together and simmer for 30 minutes. Soak meat in sauce before broiling and pour over meat as served.

SAUCE FOR CHICKEN

A little less heated in seasonings, but flavorfully effective as a marinade and basting sauce is the following:

Let chicken stand for 2 or 3 hours at room temperature in a mixture of:

- 2 parts olive oil
- 1 part wine vinegar
- 1 medium-sized onion, minced
- 1 clove garlic, minced
- Salt and pepper
- Generous pinch of tarragon, thyme, and chopped parsley

Use same mixture to baste chicken during cooking process.

CHICKEN OR TURKEY SAUCE

- 1 cup white table wine
- ¼ cup olive oil
- 2 tablespoons butter or margarine
- 1 medium onion, minced
- 1 clove garlic, crushed
- 1 teaspoon salt
- ¼ teaspoon paprika
- 2 teaspoons fresh rosemary, minced
- 1 teaspoon parsley, minced
- Freshly ground pepper

Simmer all ingredients for 15 minutes.

DUCK SAUCE

½ cube butter or margarine
2 tablespoons olive oil
2 large onions, chopped
2 cloves garlic
1 large green pepper, chopped
½ cup celery, chopped
Juice and chopped peel of ½ lemon
1 sprig fresh rosemary
½ dozen sage leaves
½ teaspoon monosodium glutamate
1 pint white or red wine

Melt the butter in frying pan with olive oil, then add all the remaining ingredients except the wine. Sauté until mixture is soft and the onions a golden brown. Just before serving the ducks, add the wine to the mixture, and bring to a boil. Pour over the ducks and serve.

MARINADE FOR POULTRY OR GAME

1 part Italian Vermouth
1 part olive oil

Combine wine and olive oil, mixing well. Mix thoroughly each time you baste.

SOY MARINADE FOR FISH

Marinate fish for 4 to 5 hours in a mixture of equal parts of soy sauce and water, with crushed garlic to taste. Garlic and soy sauce make a combination used frequently by the Japanese in their fish cookery. For added piquancy squeeze a little lemon or lime over the fish while they're cooking.

FISH SAUCE

2 cups meat or chicken stock
1 tablespoon soy sauce
1 tablespoon lemon juice
1 tablespoon Worcestershire sauce
¼ cup catsup
1 teaspoon paprika

Simmer all ingredients for 30 minutes.

FISH MARINADE

¼ cup soy sauce
¼ cup Bourbon or ½ cup Sherry wine
1 clove garlic, crushed
¼ cup salad oil (use less oil if your fish is a fat one)
½ teaspoon monosodium glutamate

Combine soy sauce, Bourbon or Sherry, well-crushed garlic, olive oil, and monosodium glutamate. Let mixture stand to blend the flavors.

SKILLET & KETTLE COOKING

BEEF

HAMBURGERS, GOURMET

1 pound ground beef
1 tablespoon onion juice
2 tablespoons cream
Butter
1 cup red wine

Combine the ground beef with the onion juice and cream. Shape into patties and sauté quickly in butter. Add the wine to the pan and cook until done, basting frequently. Serve between buns spread with parsley butter. Serves 4.

PAPRIKA HAMBURGER

Form meat into balls, brown on all sides in hot fat. Cover with sour cream, add onion, and a lot of paprika—enough to color the cream. Cook until done; serve with noodles.

GROUND BEEF STEW

Form meat into small balls, brown in hot fat. Add hot water, a package of frozen mixed vegetables; seasonings, such as garlic and onions; and tomato sauce, and cook until vegetables are done. Thicken if necessary. Dinner is ready in a matter of minutes.

BEEF BUNS

3 tablespoons chopped onion
Shortening
1 pound ground beef
1 teaspoon salt
1 can (8 oz.) tomato sauce
2 tablespoons catsup
½ teaspoon chili powder
2 tablespoons brown sugar
1 teaspoon dry mustard
3 tablespoons lemon juice
1 teaspoon cornstarch
1 cup diced celery

In a heavy skillet, sauté the chopped onion in a little shortening; add the ground beef and brown evenly, stirring occasionally to separate. When it is about half done, sprinkle with the salt and continue cooking. Blend together the tomato sauce, catsup, chili powder, brown sugar, dry mustard, lemon juice, and cornstarch. Stir into meat mixture and add the diced celery. Simmer about 10 minutes.

When ready to serve, heat slowly before dipping large spoonfuls over heated, split buns. Makes 10 to 12 generous servings.

OPEN-FACED CHEESEBURGERS

1 pound ground beef
¼ cup chopped onion
2 tablespoons shortening
Salt and pepper
1 can (8 oz.) tomato sauce
1 small can sliced or chopped mushrooms
½ cup grated cheese

Brown the ground beef with the chopped onion in shortening. Season with salt and pepper. Stir in tomato sauce and mushrooms. Simmer about 10 minutes, remove from heat and add the grated cheese, stirring well to blend.

Toast buns over coals; spoon on mixture.

SHORT RIBS

3 pounds beef shortribs
Flour
Cooking oil
Salt and pepper
1 teaspoon powdered mustard
½ teaspoon cumin (or 1 teaspoon chili pepper)
½ teaspoon chili pepper
1½ teaspoon garlic salt
1 teaspoon onion salt (or ½ cup diced onions)
1 green pepper, diced
2 large tomatoes, diced
½ cup vinegar
¾ cup brown sugar
Flour

Roll ribs in flour and brown in skillet in hot oil. After meat is browned, add salt and pepper to taste, then add all ingredients except the vinegar and sugar. Simmer for 15 minutes. Add vinegar and sugar, sprinkle enough flour over mixture to thicken it, and cook over low fire until meat is done. Serve over boiled rice. Serves 4.

MEXICAN GULACHI

- Bacon fat
- 4 pounds ground or cubed beef
- 1 medium-sized onion, chopped
- 1 green pepper, chopped
- 2 teaspoons (or more) chili powder
- 3 teaspoons prepared mustard
- 6 large onions, sliced
- Salt and pepper to taste
- 6 large potatoes, peeled and sliced
- 8 stalks celery, sliced
- 1 cup raw rice
- 1 can (No. 2) or 2½ cups cooked red kidney beans
- 1 can (10½ oz.) condensed tomato soup mixed with an equal quantity of water
- 1 can (8 oz.) tomato sauce mixed with an equal quantity of water

For this recipe you will need first a large iron kettle which can be hung over the fire in an outdoor fireplace or buried in the barbecue coals. Grease the kettle generously with bacon fat.

Mix the beef, chopped onion, green pepper, chili powder, and prepared mustard. Cover the bottom of the kettle with the sliced onions; sprinkle with salt and pepper. Over the onions arrange the potatoes; salt and pepper these, also. Cover the potatoes with the seasoned beef, then add the celery, next the rice, and last the beans. Over all pour the diluted tomato soup and tomato sauce.

Cover tightly and cook over an outdoor fire or in a barbecue pit, forgetting about it for about 4 or 5 hours. Serves 8 to 10.

VIGNERONNE

- 2 pounds lean shoulder of beef
- ½ cube butter
- 4 shallots or medium-sized onions
- 1 clove garlic
- 1 tablespoon flour (preferably whole wheat)
- 1 quart Burgundy
- 1 teaspoon salt
- ½ teaspoon EACH of black pepper, thyme, sage
- 1 small bay leaf
- ½ cup chopped bacon
- 1 dozen chopped green onions
- ½ pound sliced mushrooms or small can

Cut meat into 1½-inch cubes. Fry in deep pan, in butter, over hot coals. When well browned on outside, add the shallots, garlic, and flour, and let brown. Add wine enough to cover completely; season with salt, pepper, thyme, sage and bay leaf and simmer over low coals for about 2 hours, until meat is tender and gravy has thickened. Half hour before serving, put bacon, green onions, and mushrooms in a small frying pan and cook until nicely browned. Add to the meat, let cook for a few minutes, and serve, preferably over steamed rice. Serves 4.

SPICY ROUND STEAK

1½ pounds round steak
2 tablespoons drippings or shortening
1 bottle catsup or ½ bottle catsup and ½ bottle chili sauce
¼ cup water to rinse out catsup bottle
½-1 cup canned button mushrooms
Garlic salt, optional

Bang the steak on both sides with sharp butcher knife. Salt the steak lightly. Brown quickly on both sides in hot drippings. Place skillet on grill over low coals, put on the lid, and cook slowly until tender, turning once. While steak is cooking, simmer catsup, water, mushrooms, and garlic salt in a separate frying pan for 10 minutes, stirring frequently. When steak is tender, spoon sauce over it; continue to simmer for 15 minutes. Serves 4.

Cut very thin slices of round steak into 2-inch strips, about 4 inches long. Brush with liquid smoke, sprinkle with salt and pepper and fine-chopped onion. Roll up strips and fasten with toothpicks. Brown rolls in heated shortening, then add about ¼ cup hot water or stock, cover pan, and simmer gently for 25 to 30 minutes, or until rolls are tender.

SAUSAGE

FRANK FRITTATA

2 teaspoons butter or margarine
3 tablespoons minced onion
2 tablespoons minced green pepper
4 franks, cut across in thin slices
4 eggs
¼ cup cream
Salt and pepper to taste

Melt butter in skillet. Add onion and green pepper and cook gently for about 5 minutes. Add frank slices and brown lightly. Beat eggs, add cream, then pour into skillet. Sprinkle with salt and pepper. Cook slowly, stirring carefully until mixture starts to set. Turn out onto heated platter. Serves 3 to 4.

RED-SKINS

Put frankfurters in a large skillet and cover with canned tomatoes or tomato sauce. Sprinkle lightly with salt and dot with butter. Cook slowly at the back of the grill until the franks have burst open and the sauce has been cooked down quite thick. Serve on hot plates, with remaining sauce.

PORK

BARBECUED SLICED HAM

- 2 medium-sized ham slices, medium thick
- 1 tablespoon butter
- Garlic
- 2 tablespoons dry mustard
- 3 tablespoons brown sugar
- ½ teaspoon paprika
- 6 tablespoons Sherry

Fry ham lightly on both sides in melted butter, then rub with garlic. Combine mustard, brown sugar, paprika, and stir in Sherry. Pour this mixture over the ham and put lid on frying pan. Fry until lower side is browned. Remove lid, flip ham, and brown the other side. Remove ham to platter, pour remaining sauce from the frying pan on top of it, and it is ready to serve. Serves 4.

Here's a variation to try:

- 2 medium-sized ham slices, cut thin, or 4 small slices
- 1 tablespoon butter or margarine
- 3 tablespoons vinegar
- ½ teaspoon dry mustard
- ½ teaspoon brown sugar
- ⅛ teaspoon paprika

Fry the ham slices in melted butter or margarine until slightly brown. Put on warm platter. Add vinegar, mustard, brown sugar, and paprika to fat in pan and stir until all the brown particles are mixed in well. Pour over ham. Serve at once. You will mop up the platter, it is so good. Serves 2 to 4, depending on appetites.

PORK CHOPS

Fry 4 to 6 thick chops in skillet until done, then pour off excess fat. To ½ cup catsup, add 1 tablespoon each of sugar, vinegar, and Worcestershire sauce. Pour over chops and simmer until sauce thickens. Serves 4 to 6.

NOODLES AND PORK CHOPS

- 6 loin chops or 4 lean shoulder steaks
- 2 medium onions, sliced
- 1 half-pound package of noodles, uncooked
- 1 teaspoon A-1 sauce
- Salt and pepper
- 1 can condensed tomato soup
- 1 cup water

Brown the chops in a heavy, deep skillet with a lid, or in a Dutch oven, heated on the grill over the coals. Add the rest of the ingredients and cook very slowly for an hour on top of the grill. Add more water if it cooks dry. Serves 6.

FOWL

POULET A L'ARDENNES

1 ($2\frac{1}{2}$ to 3 pound) frying chicken
Salt and pepper
½ cup butter or margarine
2 tablespoons flour
1 bottle (⅘ quart) dry white or red wine, heated
1 clove garlic, minced
6 or 8 small whole onions
$2\frac{1}{2}$ bay leaves
3 sprigs parsley, minced

Cut chicken into pieces for serving; wash quickly and dry well. Season each piece with salt and pepper. Heat butter in a heavy skillet, then add chicken and sauté to a golden brown. Remove chicken from pan and add flour slowly to the drippings, blending well. Slowly add the wine, stirring constantly until sauce is smooth and slightly thickened. Then add garlic, onions, bay leaves, and parsley; season to taste with salt and pepper. Add the browned chicken. Cover skillet and simmer gently over a low fire for about an hour, or until the chicken has become tender.

When done, remove chicken to a heated platter; thicken wine sauce with a small amount of flour paste. Serve with rice. Serves 4.

PONED CHICKEN

Using coarse, yellow cornmeal, make batter as for corn bread, but thick.

Fry your chicken, as you choose, to tenderness. Remove from fire, and bone. Make your gravy.

Put your heavy griddle on your grill and swipe with bacon rind. When griddle is hot, drop batter on it in large "puddles" about 6 inches in diameter and ½ inch thick. When they start to "perk," put layers of the chicken on top and cover with more batter. Cook on both sides, to a golden brown crust. Serve with chicken gravy.

Menu suggestion: Serve with a generous sized ice-cold vegetable salad.

DOVES SAN JOAQUIN

10 to 15 doves
Flour
Salt and pepper
Poultry seasoning
¼ pound butter, melted
1 can (8 oz.) tomato sauce
1 medium-sized can mushroom stems and pieces
1 large onion, diced
Milk for gravy

Flour the doves by dropping 2 or 3 at a time into a paper sack in which flour and seasonings have been placed. Brown in the

melted butter, as you would frying chicken, in a large skillet. Add the tomato sauce, mushrooms, and onion; place lid on the skillet, set over coals, and cook until tender when tested with a fork. Stir birds occasionally, as they have a tendency to stick to the bottom of the pan. If the birds seem to be drying out, add ½ cup of hot water.

When done, remove birds and place in warming oven. Add milk to residue in the skillet and make milk gravy. Serve with hot biscuits and tossed salad. Serves 10.

Variation: Substitute Sherry for the tomato sauce. Add it when the doves are about half cooked.

DUTCH OVEN SQUAB

- 6 whole squabs
- 2 cans hominy
- 1 teaspoon salt
- ½ teaspoon pepper
- 1 tablespoon paprika
- 1 sprig sweet basil
- Butter
- 1 cup Claret
- Additional paprika
- Chopped parsley

Clean the squabs. Boil the livers, gizzards, and hearts in salted water until tender; drain and chop them fine; add the drained hominy, salt, pepper, paprika, and sweet basil. Stuff the mixture into the squabs and sew up. Then sear them in a lightly buttered Dutch oven until brown. Baste with the wine and cook over a medium fire for 30 minutes, adding a little water if necessary to prevent burning. Sprinkle each squab with paprika and chopped parsley and serve on individual plates. Season and thicken the pan gravy, and serve separately. This should be poured over the hominy when the squabs are opened at the table.

PHEASANT DELIGHT

- 1 pheasant
- Flour
- Olive oil
- 2 onions, minced
- 2 green peppers, minced
- 1 clove garlic, minced
- Few sprigs of parsley, minced
- Pinch of rosemary, marjoram, sage, and thyme
- 1 cup hot water

Cut pheasant in small pieces, strip breast meat from the bones. Dip in flour, season with salt and pepper. Brown in olive oil.

When brown, remove pheasant from oil. Add minced onions, pepper, garlic, herbs, and hot water to oil, and stir until well blended. Return pheasant to pan, cover, and simmer for 1 hour. Remove bird, thicken gravy, and add dumplings. Serve on large platter surrounded by dumplings and garnishes. Serves 6.

PAN-FRIED TROUT

Clean trout and wipe completely dry. Dip each trout in light cream, then roll in a mixture of half flour and half cornmeal, well seasoned with salt and pepper. (Seasoned flour or cracker meal may also be used for coating the fish.) Be sure the pan for frying is large enough so that the fish won't touch one another during cooking. Use enough oil (peanut oil is good) to keep the fish from sticking and burning. When the oil is hot, but not smoking, gently lay in the coated trout. Fry quickly to a crisp, crackly, golden brown on one side, then turn the fish with a broad spatula and brown on the other side. During the short cooking period, keep the oil bubbling hot, but take care that it does not burn. Remove the trout to a heated platter and garnish with crisp, fresh watercress and peeled orange segments that have been quickly sautéed in butter. Spread the following Watercress Butter over the fish:

WATERCRESS BUTTER

2 to 3 tablespoons finely chopped fresh watercress leaves
4 tablespoons softened butter or margarine
Few drops strained lemon juice

Blend ingredients together well.

FRESH MACKEREL

Clean, split, and bone the mackerel, but leave the skin of the back intact. Sprinkle liberally with paprika, and fry, meat side down, in a pan with the bottom barely covered with equal parts of olive oil and melted butter. Turn the fish over when done, sprinkle the meat side with salt and pepper, squeeze on some lemon juice, and baste with the drippings before serving. Flank with a generous mound of mashed potatoes with a dimple in the top, and fill the dimple with pan gravy.

VENISON

DEER LIVER

Cut liver in thin slices, and let stand in a mixture of equal parts of vinegar and water for 30 minutes. Drain and wipe dry. Dip each piece of liver in flour that has been seasoned with salt and pepper. Heat some deer fat, and in it sauté a finely sliced onion to a golden brown; over this rub two pieces of garlic together until the juice runs into the sauce. Sauté liver slices in a separate pan. When brown and cooked on both sides (5 or 6 minutes cooking time), add the onion-garlic sauce and serve.

MULLIGAN STEW

No one should go through the venison season without experiencing at least one mulligan stew. For this you can use the least tender parts of the venison. Trim and cut in small pieces, sprinkle with salt and flour, and sizzle in hot fat (preferably half butter) until well browned; then place it in your Dutch oven or whatever you use for stews. Rinse out every drop of the gravy from the frying pan and pour over the meat in the cooker, cover, and let cook slowly about 1½ hours. Then add the vegetables. Onions, carrots, string beans and tomatoes are the best. Fresh corn cut from the cob may be added, too. It's only a matter of choice about cutting up the vegetables. At any rate, add them all to the partly cooked meat, sprinkle with salt and add enough water to fill about half full. Cover tightly and cook slowly for about 45 minutes.

A little while before you are ready to serve, remove all the vegetables and meat, thicken the gravy slightly, and season it to taste. If you have ½ cup of sour cream to add at this time, nothing makes this stew better! Then return the vegetables and meat to the gravy and keep all very hot until ready to serve.

VENISON HUNTER'S STYLE

3 pounds of venison
Salt and pepper
2 tablespoons butter
1 onion, chopped
1 1-inch cube of ham
1 clove garlic, minced
2 bay leaves
2 sprigs thyme
1 tablespoon flour
2 cups warm water
1 quart consomme
½ pound fresh mushrooms chopped
Grated peel of 1 lemon

Cut the venison into pieces 2 inches square. Salt and pepper generously. Put the butter into the skillet with the venison and let the meat brown slowly. When it is nearly brown, add the chopped onion and let it brown slightly. Then add the ham, garlic, bay leaves, and thyme, all minced very fine. Stir and simmer for 2 minutes. Add the flour and cook a few minutes longer. Add the warm water and let come to a good simmer. Now add the consomme and let all cook slowly for 1 hour. Season again according to taste and add the mushrooms and the lemon peel. Let all cook a ½ hour longer and serve on very hot plates. Serves 8.

VENISON HAMBURGER DELICIOUS

- 2 pounds venison
- 1 medium-sized onion
- 3 eggs
- ½ cup cream
- 1 cup stale bread crumbs
- 2 teaspoons salt
- 2 teaspoons sage
- ¼ teaspoon black pepper
- A dash of cayenne

Put the venison and onion through food chopper. Add eggs (beaten), crumbs, cream and seasonings. Mix well and form into patties. Roll in flour and fry in plenty of sizzling hot fat until well done. Put onto a hot platter, dot with butter and serve at once. These are good also when dropped into tomato sauce to which has been added a little A-1. Simmer 30-40 minutes in this sauce. Serves 8.

CORNED BEEF HASH, YANKEE STYLE

- 4 to 5 pounds brisket of corned beef, cooked
- 4 or 5 tablespoons fat
- 6 large white onions, diced
- 6 large potatoes, boiled, peeled, and diced
- 1 can (No. 2½) diced beets
- 1 clove garlic, crushed
- 2 tablespoons butter or margarine
- Salt and pepper to taste

Remove excess fat from corned beef, and mince the meat with a sharp knife. Melt fat in a large, heavy skillet; add onions and sauté until they are tender and golden. Gradually add corned beef and then potatoes, stirring constantly. Slowly stir in beets and beet juice. Last, add garlic and butter. Allow the mixture to simmer gently until it's good and hot and bubbly. Before serving, taste and add salt and pepper as necessary. (Garlic can be removed before serving, if desired.)

Serves 6 to 8 people, but if your guests are hash addicts, better count on serving about 4.

STEWS, ETC.

SLUMGULLION

A barbecue-grill dish that tastes like more:

- 4 slices bacon, cut in squares
- 1 onion
- 1 can tomatoes
- ¼ pound cheese
- ½ pound meat (you can use your leftovers or fresh meat)

Brown bacon and onions together. Add tomatoes and meat which has been cut into small pieces. Simply add the cheese, which has been diced, and when it's melted you have a barbecue delight that can be served on toasted and buttered sour French bread. Serves 6.

COWBOY CORN

¼ pound bacon or salt pork, diced
2 cans (No. 2) whole kernel corn
1 green pepper, finely chopped
Onion, celery, garlic, chili powder, and pepper to taste

Fry the bacon or salt pork lightly. Drain the juice from the canned corn and save this liquor to use later. Dump the corn into the hot skillet and let it sizzle for two or three minutes before stirring. Drop into this the green pepper (or red pepper if you want it hot) and other seasonings. When everything is mixed thoroughly, empty the corn liquor into the pan. If this doesn't furnish enough moisture, add fresh or evaporated milk. Let it simmer, with a top on the pan, until liquid substances have almost disappeared. With tortillas replacing silverware, you'll have a real taste treat. Serves 6.

CHUCK-WAGON STEW

3 or 4 pounds beef, inch-size chunks
1 can (No. 2½) solid pack tomatoes
3 or 4 onions, diced
Salt and pepper

Put pan, heavy Dutch-oven type, on fire with enough fat to cover the bottom. Sear beef over hot fire. Stir to avoid burning. Add tomatoes, onions, salt, and pepper. Simmer 2 hours, adding water from time to time for liquid for gravy. When meat is tender, stir in enough flour, about 2 tablespoons—blended with a little water before adding—to thicken slightly.

Serve this stew with rice and any vegetables you wish, but don't forget the beans and plenty of coffee. You can doctor up the dish with a bay leaf, a pinch of thyme, and garlic if you like. Serves 6.

CORN CHOWDER

Steaming corn chowder can be cooked quickly and easily in a skillet over your barbecue grill. Here's how:

4 slices bacon
2 medium-sized onions
3 medium-sized potatoes
3 cups water
1 teaspoon salt
1 can (No. 2½) corn
1 can tomato soup
1 small can evaporated milk

After the bacon has been cut into small pieces and browned, add finely chopped onions. Return to grill and brown slightly. To this mixture, add sliced potatoes, water and salt. Cook until potato bits are tender; then add corn and tomato soup. Boil for a few minutes and add milk. If you like, you may add cubes of ham and cook a few more minutes. Serves 3 or 4.

SKILLET GOULASH

½ pound bacon, diced
1 can (No. 2) whole kernel corn
1 can (No. 2½) tomatoes
1 large onion, chopped
1 raw potato, chopped
Salt and pepper
A little water

Fry the bacon in a heavy skillet until you have a good amount of melted fat, then add the other ingredients. Cook for 20 to 30 minutes. Serves 6.

PASSOLI

Here's a meal-in-one-kettle, perfect to serve with boiled rice and a green salad for a barbecue supper.

2 pounds lean pork, cubed
¼ cup shortening
Salt and pepper
3 medium onions, chopped
1 or more cloves garlic
1 green pepper, chopped
1 can (No. 2½) tomatoes
1 can (6 oz.) tomato paste
Water
3 tablespoons chili powder
1 can (No. 2½) hominy, drained
1 can pimientos or green chilis, chopped
2 to 4 tablespoons flour

Brown the cubes of meat on all sides in the hot shortening in a large, heavy kettle, sprinkling the meat with salt and pepper while turning it. Add the chopped onion, garlic, and pepper and cook until they are limp and slightly browned. Add the tomatoes, tomato paste, and enough water to cover. Let simmer gently for 4 hours, adding more water from time to time if it looks at all dry. Mix the chili powder with a little cold water and stir into the mixture. Add the drained hominy and chopped pimientos or chilis. Taste to see if more salt is needed. Mix the flour with a little water to form a thin paste, add slowly to the hot mixture, stirring constantly, and cook, stirring, until smoothly thickened. Boil 20 minutes longer and serve piping hot. Serves 8.

VEGETABLE DISHES

CHILI FANDANGO

2 bell peppers
¼ pound sliced bacon, diced
1 onion, minced
1 clove garlic, minced
4 large tomatoes, peeled and diced
¼ teaspoon salt

Toast bell peppers over coals until black. Scrape off black skins, and cut each pepper into 3 or 4 pieces. Fry bacon, onion, and garlic together until crisp and brown. Add peppers, tomatoes, and salt. Cook slowly in covered pan for 35 minutes. Serves 6.

GARDEN BOUQUET

1 can (No. 2½) tomatoes
1 tablespoon butter
Salt and pepper to taste
1 tablespoon sugar
1 cup celery
3 tablespoons parsley (packed)

Heat tomatoes steaming hot, not boiling. Add butter, salt, pepper, and sugar. Last, add the celery, chopped fine, and chopped parsley. Serve at once. Serves 4.

TOMATOES AND PEPPERS

Wash bell peppers (allow 2 or 3 per person) and soak in ice water for an hour; then dice in about inch squares, discarding the coarse membrane and seeds. Cook in several tablespoons of hot olive oil until soft and slightly browned. Pour off all excess oil and add as much peeled and chopped tomatoes as there are peppers. Season with salt and pepper. Push to back of grill and cook slowly for 20 to 30 minutes. Serve as a side dish with barbecued meats.

SAUTÉED CARROTS CHATEAU

1 tablespoon butter or other shortening
2 cups carrots, diced and cooked until tender
1½ cups California Tokay or Angelica
2 tablespoons lemon juice
Salt and pepper to taste

Melt butter in frying pan and allow carrots to sauté slowly until slightly browned. Combine wine and lemon juice and pour over carrots. Simmer slowly until candied, and season to taste. Serves 4.

RISOTTO A LA RATTO

1 small yellow onion, chopped
2 tablespoons butter or margarine
1 cup uncooked white rice
4 cups clear chicken broth
1 can (4 oz.) button mushrooms
Salt to taste
½ teaspoon saffron
½ cup grated Parmesan-type cheese

Sauté onion in butter until transparent but not brown. Add rice and stir until each grain is coated with the butter. Add 1 cup boiling chicken broth and cook over low fire, stirring frequently, until rice has absorbed liquid. Repeat process with remaining broth, adding 1 cup at a time as rice absorbs it. (This will take about 20 minutes.) Add mushrooms and salt, then stir in saffron which has been dissolved in 1 tablespoon hot water or broth. Cook 5 minutes longer. Blend in the grated cheese, and serve at once.

PILAFF

Pilaff makes an excellent rice accompaniment for shish kebabs and may be eaten with or without the sauce. If you wish to use wheat instead of rice, go to an Armenian store and ask for pilaff Bulghour. There are three grinds and this will get you the right kind. In the recipe simply substitute Bulghour for rice and go on from there. A lot of people feel that rice is best with fowl and wheat with meats, but there is no rule.

BROTH FOR PILAFF

For 6 to 8 persons make 1 quart of broth. Cover with water the lamb bones and trimmings left over after making shish kebab. Season with vegetables and herbs. After the broth cooks down, strain before using in the pilaff.

PREPARATION OF PILAFF

For 6 to 8 people. If you want more or less, simply change the amounts to suit as long as the proportions of the ingredients one to the other remain the same.

- 2 cups rice or Bulghour (do not wash)
- 1 cup fine noodles
- 4 tablespoons butter (½ cube)
- 4 cups boiling broth

Use long grained white rice. Buy barley noodles from an Armenian or Italian store. If you can't get them, use the thinnest egg noodles obtainable and crush them until they are all broken into small pieces about ½ inch long or less.

Brown the noodles in the butter until tan, pour in the rice, and mix well. The rice should not fry but merely become covered with the butter. Pour over it the boiling broth, cover, and allow to simmer slowly without stirring for 20 minutes or until all broth has simmered away. It can be reheated by adding a little water and steaming for a short time. Variations can be made with different kinds of broth and different kinds of fat. Chicken fat and broth make excellent pilaff.

BROWN RICE PILAFF

Fry 1 cup of uncooked brown rice in 3 tablespoons of oil in a large skillet. Stir it constantly until it turns a golden brown. Then season it and pour on enough soup stock or canned bouillon to cover. (This should take slightly more than 2 cups.) Cover the pan and simmer over a slow fire until all the liquid is absorbed and the rice is almost dry. Then top it with butter and serve. Serves 4.

PINTO BEANS RANCH STYLE

- 1 pound pinto beans
- 1 good-sized onion, sliced
- ¼ teaspoon chili powder
- 1 can (No. 2½) solid pack tomatoes
- ½ cup brown sugar or honey
- 1 slice (5-inch) very smoky bacon rind

Pick beans over, cover with cold water and let stand overnight. Next morning, drain and cover with boiling water. Boil steadily 1 hour. Pour off water, and re-cover with boiling water so that about 2 inches of water shows above the level of the beans. Boil steadily 1 hour, then add bacon rind, salt, and pepper to taste. Continue boiling 1 hour more, then add remaining ingredients. Cook 2 or 3 hours longer. They will be good any time from then on and can be heated on the grill whenever they are needed. More water may be added from time to time, in order not to burn the thick soup that accumulates. Old fashioned pink beans may be used, but they must be cooked 2 hours longer. Serves 10.

MEXICAN BEANS

- 2 cups (1 pound) pink beans
- 2 large onions, sliced
- 2 cloves garlic
- 2 teaspoons salt
- ½ pound fresh pork (side meat)
- ½ pound boneless beef stew meat
- 1 can tomato sauce
- 1 can water
- ½ teaspoon black pepper
- ¼ teaspoon oregano
- ¼ teaspoon Mexican sage
- ¼ teaspoon cumin seed
- 1½ to 2 tablespoons chili powder

Pick over the beans and let them soak overnight in water to cover. In the morning drain, cover with fresh water, and boil 15 minutes. Drain and again cover with plenty of fresh water; add 1 onion, sliced; 1 clove of garlic, minced fine; and 1 teaspoon of salt. Put on to cook slowly. While the beans are simmering, dice the fresh pork fine, put into skillet with a teaspoon of shortening and brown nicely. Cut the beef into small cubes, add these to the pork, and brown lightly. Put in the other onion, sliced, and the other clove of garlic, minced, and continue cooking until the onion is tender but not brown. Add the tomato sauce and water, the pepper, salt and other seasonings, and let cook for about 5 minutes. Then turn the mixture into a kettle with the beans, and let boil slowly about 2½ hours, or until the beans are thoroughly tender. Warm up or finish cooking on the grill. Taste to see that seasonings are right and add more salt if necessary. More water may be added from time to time while the beans are cooking if they appear to be getting dry. Serves 4 to 6.

MEXICAN BEANS—SIMPLER VERSION

1 pint red beans
1½ cloves garlic
2 medium onions, chopped
3 green peppers
2 teaspoons salt
½ teaspoon black pepper
1 tablespoon bacon fat

Wash and soak beans for several hours, then boil gently for 2 hours. Drain and rinse. Put fat in skillet; add chopped onion, garlic, peppers, salt and pepper; let cook 5 minutes; then add to beans in pot with enough water to cover. Let boil slowly until thoroughly soft, but not mushy. Add hot water if necessary during the cooking. Warm up or finish cooking on the grill.

SPANISH STYLE BEANS

1 pound Mexican red or pink beans
2 large onions, minced
3 cloves garlic
⅓ cup olive oil
Salt and freshly ground pepper

Soak the beans overnight and cook in the same water. After the beans have cooked about 1 hour, add the onions, garlic, olive oil, salt and pepper. Cook until done, then take out about ½ cup of beans, pulverize them and return to thicken the sauce. Simmer until the sauce is of the proper consistency—not too thick, but not runny. Warm up or finish cooking on the grill.

POTATOES KAILUA

Take good-sized potatoes and boil in their jackets for 5 or 6 minutes. Drain. Put a cup of bacon fat or oil in your Dutch oven and place on grill. When the oil or fat is hot, toss in a teaspoon of whole allspice and 10 or 12 whole cloves. Roll each potato in the hot fat or oil until coated, then stack them in and put the lid on tight. Push the Dutch oven to back of grill. Takes about 30 minutes for potatoes to cook through.

FRIED POTATO PEELS

(Kitchen recipe.) Here is a fresh way to serve potatoes to accompany grilled lamb, veal or beef. Ask your favorite restaurant to save you a batch of fresh potato peelings. Pick them up on your way home and don't loiter or they'll discolor. Wash. Dry. Have your deep fat HOT. Fill your frying basket full and fry until peels are crisp and chewy. Drain them on absorbent paper and dust with salt, coarsely ground pepper, and garlic powder before serving.

PANCAKES

POTATO PANCAKES

6 medium-sized, raw potatoes
1 onion
2 eggs, beaten
2 tablespoons flour
1 tablespoon milk
1 teaspoon salt
Pepper
Oil or bacon drippings

Grate the potatoes and onion; mix in the eggs, flour, milk, salt, and pepper, and add a little oil or bacon drippings. Shape into flat cakes 2 or 3 inches across, and pan-fry to a golden brown. Serves 6.

SOUR-DOUGH PANCAKES

Here's how to make pancakes the pioneer way, without benefit of prepared mixes.

3 cups flour
4 cups water
1 tablespoon sugar
1 cake dry yeast

First step is to make the "starter" batch. Use a wooden bucket or a crock with a loose-fitting cover. Mix the flour with the water until smooth. Add the sugar and the yeast cake, which has been soaked in ¼ cup of water. Stir the whole mass together in the bucket; then place the cover loosely on top. It is important that cover be loose-fitting. Place the bucket in a spot where it will be protected from temperature extremes. During a cold night, the activity of the yeast will be retarded, but the yeast cells will not necessarily die.

Now for the pancakes: In the evening add enough flour to make a little more batter than you intend to use the next morning. Make the batter pretty thin. If you keep the bucket in a warm place during the night, you will find the sour-dough has risen and thickened to a light, frothy mass by morning.

When ready to fry the flapjacks, pour about 1 pint of the sour-dough into a mixing pan (leaving some to go on "working") and stir in:

1 egg
1 tablespoon sugar
½ teaspoon salt
½ teaspoon soda

Beat well. Fry the pancakes in a large iron skillet, well greased, over low coals. Makes about 10 pancakes.

To keep the starter going, just add flour and water to the left-over starter to make a little more batter than you will need the next day.

OVEN ROASTING

BEEF A LA STEWART

Place a well-aged piece of top sirloin, weighing not less than 4 pounds, in a roasting pan and marinate for 24 hours with the following mixture:

2 cloves garlic, finely chopped
1 tablespoon Worcestershire sauce
Pepper, freshly ground
Salt
3 medium onions, finely chopped
½ bottle spicy catsup

The meat should be turned over at least once during the marinating and the marinade spread evenly over it.

Just before putting the meat in the oven, pour over it ½ cup Sherry. Roast in a very hot oven (500°) for about 45 minutes, or until medium rare. Hot water will have to be added once or twice during the cooking in order that the condiments on the bottom of the pan do not burn. Just before removing the roast from the oven, pour a little more Sherry over it.

After the meat is removed from the pan, make sauce by adding hot water and a small amount of catsup to the ingredients left in the pan. Bring sauce to a brisk boil, stirring vigorously. If a thinner sauce is desired, proceed as above, but strain before serving.

SIRLOIN STEAK À LA "SOY"

1 sirloin or porterhouse steak
3½ or 4 inches thick
1¼ cups soy sauce
1 tablespoon powdered mustard
3 cups granulated sugar
4 or 5 giant white onions

Rub steak with garlic and place in roasting pan into which has been poured ¾ cup of soy sauce with mustard stirred in. Soak steak in sauce on each side for about 5 minutes. Now sprinkle on 1 side of steak 1½ cups sugar and smother with half-inch-thick slices of onion. Place pan (without cover, of course) under broiler, medium flame, so that the meat is about 5 inches away from the flame. Baste well with the soy sauce about every 5 or 7 minutes. After about 35 minutes take out of broiler, brush aside onions, which will be charred, turn the steak over, cover with remaining sugar and onions as before and add balance of soy sauce. Replace in broiler and cook as before for 35 minutes, continuing basting. Remove and brush aside onions and sugared crust. Serve. The meat will be very rare but even the "medium-well" steak eater will come back for more. There is no trace of sweetness imparted to the meat from the sugar.

BREAST OF LAMB

2 pounds breast of lamb
Salt and pepper to taste
1 lemon, thinly sliced
1 large onion, finely chopped
1 cup catsup
1 cup water
3 tablespoons vinegar
3 tablespoons brown sugar
1 teaspoon chili powder
2 tablespoons Worcestershire sauce

Cut breast of lamb into serving-sized pieces; spread in a shallow casserole or baking pan; season generously with salt and pepper. Place a slice of lemon on each piece of meat; sprinkle onion over all. Bake, uncovered, in a hot oven (450°) 30 minutes to brown well. While meat is browning, combine remaining ingredients in a small saucepan; bring to boil and cook for about 5 minutes. Pour sauce over browned meat; cover casserole or pan. Reduce oven temperature to moderate (350°) and bake for 1 hour longer. Serves 4.

LITTLE PIG POTATOES

With a coring knife cut out the centers of medium large potatoes. Stuff a small sausage in the hole. Seal both ends with pieces of the potato core. If you like your sausages brown, this core can be removed toward the last. Bake in barbecue oven.

OVEN-BARBECUED SPARERIBS

3 pounds of spareribs
2 onions, sliced
2 tablespoons vinegar
2 tablespoons Worcestershire sauce
1 teaspoon salt
1 teaspoon paprika
¼ teaspoon cayenne
½ teaspoon black pepper
1 teaspoon chili powder
¾ cup ketchup
¾ cup water

Select meaty spareribs and either cut in pieces or leave whole. Sprinkle with salt and pepper, place in a roaster and cover with sliced onions. Combine remaining ingredients to make sauce, and pour over meat. Cover and bake in a moderate oven (350°) for 1½ to 2 hours, basting frequently and turning meat once or twice to brown nicely. Remove cover from roaster during last 20 minutes for extra browning. Serves 6.

SPICY SPARERIBS

Cut about 5 pounds of lean pork spareribs into suitable pieces, and brown them on your barbecue grill. But first prepare the following sauce:

Chop medium fine: 1 cup parsley, 3 large green peppers, 5 large onions, and 1 clove of garlic. Add this to a can (No. 10) of tomatoes, and place all on the stove to boil. While it is bubbling up, add:

2 teaspoons ground cloves
2 teaspoons ground cinnamon
2 teaspoons ground allspice
4 teaspoons celery seed
4 teaspoons celery salt
1½ cups tarragon vinegar
2 cups white sugar
2 teaspoons red coloring
¼ cup minced canned pimientos
Salt to taste

Cook for one hour, and, while hot, run the mixture through a coarse sieve, or food mill. Pour over the browned spareribs, and place in a 400° oven. Be sure and put them in a covered pan or roaster. Bake for 1½ hours. When done, pour ½ cup of sweet Sherry over them. Serve at once. Serves 5 to 6.

CHINESE-OVEN PIG (SUI GEE)

Take an 18 to 20-pound pig, remove most of the shoulder bones, and split the chine bone down the back from the inside, taking care not to cut the outer skin. Replace the shoulder blade and pelvis bone with bamboo sticks so the pig won't lose its shape. Rub salt and pepper and a barbecue sauce with a catsup base in the cavities, wire the pig, and hang in the oven which has been preheated so the masonry walls are very hot. Put the cover in place and cook for ½ hour. Remove the pig and puncture holes

through the skin with an ice pick over the entire surface of the animal to allow some of the fat and juices to escape. Wash with hot water to which a little honey has been added, return to the oven and cook until done, usually 1 to 2 hours. Seal lid of oven with wet sacks to retain heat.

SMOKED CHOPS IN CASSEROLE

Salt and pepper
4 pork or lamb shoulder chops
¾ cup solid pack tomatoes
Tomato juice, or water

Sprinkle salt and pepper on chops, and brush generously with liquid smoke. Arrange in a shallow casserole, and pour tomatoes, tomato juice, or water over the chops. Cover casserole and bake at 350° for about 1 hour, or until meat is tender. Uncover and bake for 15 minutes longer or until the meat is well browned. Chops may be baked in barbecue sauce if desired. Serves 4.

FOIL-BAKED CHICKEN

Have a fryer cut into serving-size pieces, dividing the breast into 4 servings. Allow 2 or 3 pieces of chicken a serving, reserving back, neck, and giblets for other uses. Lightly brown unfloured chicken in butter or shortening. Remove and arrange on pieces of foil. In the drippings, sauté lightly 3 small onions and 3 mushrooms per serving. Arrange these over the chicken. Sprinkle with salt, pepper, paprika, chopped parsley, and any desired herbs such as rosemary or tarragon. Pour 2 tablespoons light cream over each serving. Wrap tightly in the foil. Place in a shallow pan and bake in a hot oven (425°) for 1 hour. Longer cooking often seems to improve the flavor, if heat is reduced to low after the first hour.

QUAIL, ROASTED

Clean and wipe the birds well. Brush inside and out with butter and sprinkle inside lightly with salt and pepper. Truss the birds and bind each around with a strip of bacon. Put a little butter in a roasting pan, set the birds in the pan, and cook in hot oven for 20 or 30 minutes, according to size. Have ready as many slices of buttered toast as there are quail, place these on a hot dish, and lay a bird on each slice. Add a little butter to the gravy in which the birds have been roasted, also a little consomme and lemon juice. Let this simmer for 3 or 4 minutes, then strain and pour over the breasts of the birds so that it will soak into the toast. Garnish with thin slices of lemon and watercress, and serve.

COQ AU VIN

1 medium-sized fryer
Salt and pepper
1/3 cup butter or margarine
1 cup Claret or Burgundy
1 large onion, minced
1 small can mushroom pieces

Clean and wash fowl and cut in pieces; rub with salt and pepper. Brown in butter on all sides in heavy frying pan. Transfer chicken and drippings to casserole. Add wine, onion, and drained mushrooms. Simmer until tender, about 1 hour for a young bird. Allow 1/2 to 3/4 pound per portion.

CHINESE-OVEN DUCK

Wash the duck and tie the vent. Pour spiced soup or broth through the neck opening to practically fill the cavity. Then tie the neck. Wash in warm water to which a tablespoon of honey has been added, and allow to stand in open air to dry thoroughly. When dry, hang in the Chinese oven, which has been preheated so that it is slightly warm, and cook for about 1 1/2 hours. Steam inside the duck will make it swell up to the size of a football. The pressure helps tenderize the meat. The honey on the outside of the skin makes it brown readily and become deliciously crisp.

OVEN-BARBECUED RABBIT

2 rabbits, cut in serving size pieces
Salt and pepper
Tabasco sauce
1/8 teaspoon EACH cinnamon, allspice, and garlic salt
1/2 teaspoon paprika
3 small mint leaves
3 tablespoons chopped parsley (or 1 tablespoon parsley flakes)
2 cups water
2 tablespoons melted butter
Juice of one lemon

Season rabbit with salt and pepper and place in one layer, meaty side up, in uncovered baking pan. Shake 1 or 2 drops of Tabasco on each piece. Mix together the cinnamon, allspice, garlic salt and paprika, and sprinkle over rabbit, along with minced mint leaves and parsley. Add water. Bake in a hot oven (400°), basting frequently with the melted butter mixed with the lemon juice. Baste with juice in the pan when lemon butter runs out. Cook for 1 hour, or until tender. The liquor in the pan may be thickened for gravy. Serves 8.

FOIL-BAKED SOLE

Place sole filets on square of aluminum foil. Scatter cleaned, whole shrimp and sautéed mushrooms over the fish. Spoon a

rich white sauce, seasoned with lemon juice, over each individual portion. Sprinkle generously with chopped parsley. Bring the two edges of the foil together up over the fish and double-fold to make a tight seal. Double-fold outer edges also so that a tight, square bag or packet is formed. Place these packets on a cooky sheet and bake in a hot oven (400) for 20 minutes. To serve, snip through foil with scissors to form a criss-cross on top. Turn back the foil to make an opening. Do not remove the foil.

FOIL-BAKED SALMON

1 salmon filet
1 slice dry onion
1 bay leaf
1 slice lemon
Few peppercorns
Dash of salt

Place the salmon filet in the center of a sheet of aluminum foil, top with the onion, bay leaf, lemon, peppercorns, and salt. Wrap the foil around the fish. Place on a shallow pan and bake at 350° for 15 minutes. Remove, cool, and refrigerate overnight.

BARBECUED CRAB

Clean cooked crabs; crack legs and break body into 2 or 3 pieces. Place in baking pan or individual serving casseroles, cover with sauce (recipe on page 48), and heat over coals for about 20 minutes or until hot. Pour sauce over hot crab, and serve. Sauce may also be served in separate bowl for dunking. To garnish individual servings, place a large crab claw in center of the casserole with a stuffed olive or tomato or lime wedge grasped in the claw.

TROUT IN ENVELOPES

Trout
Salad oil or melted butter
Salt and pepper
Strained lemon juice
White wine or mushroom liquor (optional)

Brush each trout with oil or melted butter. Season inside and out with salt, pepper, and a sprinkling of lemon juice. Lay each trout in the center of a well-buttered oblong of parchment cooking paper. Add 1 tablespoon white wine or mushroom liquor to each package, if desired. Fold each oblong of paper to make a compact package and to hold in the contents. Place side by side in uncovered shallow baking pan. Do not turn packages during cooking. Bake in a hot oven (400°) about 25 minutes. Serve trout in envelopes.

BAKED STUFFED TROUT

- 3 tablespoons minced parsley
- 4 tablespoons minced onion
- ½ cup sliced, canned mushrooms
- ⅓ cup butter or margarine
- 3 cups soft, stale, white bread crumbs
- Salt and pepper
- 6 trout

Sauté the parsley, onion, and mushrooms in butter until soft, but not browned. Toss together lightly with bread crumbs to mix all ingredients. Season to taste with salt and pepper. Stuff cavity of each trout, and place in greased shallow baking pan or dish. Brush exposed surface of fish lightly with melted butter or oil. Bake in a hot oven (400°) 25 to 30 minutes. Send to the table on a heated platter. Serves 6.

BIKINI BAKED FISH

- 1¼ cups packaged coconut
- ¾ cup coffee cream
- 1½ to 2 pounds halibut, whitefish, or any other mild-flavored fish
- 1 teaspoon salt
- Several young banana leaves or fresh corn husks

Soak the coconut in cream for ½ hour. Simmer for 10 minutes and strain through several thicknesses of cheesecloth, squeezing out as much cream as possible. Scale and clean the fish and cut to fit inside leaves selected. (If corn husks are used, keep the stem and sheaves intact in removing from the ear of corn.) Place fish inside leaves, pour in the coconut cream, and tie ends with strips of leaf or husk. Place in a pan and bake at 350° about 1 to 1½ hours. Swab the husks with water from time to time, turning occasionally, to prevent burning.

WEST INDIES OVEN FISH

- One whole dolphin, of 4 to 8 pounds, or any other desired fish
- Garlic
- Salt and pepper
- Butter
- Celery seed
- Bacon strips

Clean and skin fish; remove head and tail. Rub fish with garlic; sprinkle with salt, pepper, and celery seed. Lay bacon strips close together across top of fish. Bring oven to 250° temperature and place fish in oven. Cook at 250° for 20 minutes, then allow temperature to come down to 200° and cook for about 1 hour, depending on size of fish. While the fish is cooking, baste occasionally with sauce made as follows: Mash some garlic and pour boiling water over the garlic; add salt, pepper, and butter to taste. Fish will come apart easily at the backbone and the two halves can be laid on the serving platter and garnished.

SADDLE OF VENISON

5 pound venison saddle	Salt
1 large carrot	Butter
1 large onion	½ cup consomme

Skin the saddle of venison and remove all sinews from the surface. Take fine larding needles and lard closely. Tie the saddle around with a cord 4 times. Slice the carrot and the onion into a roasting pan. Place venison on top of these, sprinkle lightly with salt, and spread with butter. Set in hot oven and roast for 40 minutes, basting frequently with pan gravy. When done, remove the binding cord, and place on hot platter.

Make gravy by pouring the consomme into the pan gravy and bringing to a boil. Skim fat off gravy, and strain over venison. Serve with hot Currant Jelly Sauce made as follows: Take 1 cup of currant jelly, blend with melted butter, and stir until jelly is dissolved. Put in a saucepan, combine with some of the venison gravy, and bring to a boil.

FIESTA ROLLS

12 French rolls	4 hard-cooked eggs, finely cut
¾ pound Cheddar cheese, cut in small pieces	2 cans (8 oz.) Spanish-style tomato sauce
1 pint pitted ripe olives	4 tablespoons wine vinegar
3 green onions, finely chopped	1 cup olive oil
3 green peppers, chopped	Salt and pepper to taste

Cut tops off all 12 rolls. Scoop out soft part in both tops and bottoms. Butter inside of tops well.

Mix all ingredients thoroughly, adding liquid ingredients last, and taking special care that the filling is not too sloppy. It may be advisable to cut down on the amount of olive oil. Fill the rolls generously. Replace buttered tops and wrap rolls in wax paper, twisting the ends closed. Bake in moderate oven on a cooky sheet about ½ hour. Allow 15 minutes for the rolls to cool before serving so they will be easier to handle without danger of burned fingers and tongues. Wrapped in wax paper, they will hold the heat.

SMOKY BEANS

Stir about a teaspoonful of liquid smoke into each pound of beans which have been prepared for baking. For quick baked beans, season canned baked beans with a small amount of liquid smoke, then place in a bean pot with a good-sized onion buried in the center. Strip bacon across the top. Bake in a moderate oven (375°) for about 45 minutes.

MACARONI AND CHEESE

1½ cups elbow macaroni, uncooked
¼ cup butter
1½ cups American cheese
1½ tablespoons parsley
1½ tablespoons pimiento
1½ tablespoons onion
1 teaspoon salt
⅛ teaspoon pepper
½ teaspoon paprika
2 eggs
2 cups milk

Cook the macaroni in boiling salted water for 15 minutes. Drain and pour cold water through it. Put it in a buttered baking dish. Add the butter, cubed cheese, chopped onion, parsley, pimiento and seasonings to the macaroni. Beat the eggs slightly and add milk to them. Pour over the macaroni and cheese and bake, uncovered, at 325° for 50 minutes. This may be served with mushroom sauce. Serves 6.

MACARONI BAKE

2 cups shell macaroni
1 cup cottage cheese
1 cup sour cream
1 clove garlic, minced
1 medium sized onion, minced
2 tablespoons Worcestershire sauce
1 tablespoon chili sauce
2 drops Tabasco sauce
Salt and pepper to taste
Grated Parmesan cheese

Cook macaroni in boiling salted water until just tender. Drain, and rinse with cold water. Place in bowl and combine with cottage cheese, sour cream, garlic, onion, Worcestershire sauce, chili sauce, Tabasco sauce, salt, and pepper. Turn into a greased casserole and bake at 350° for about 45 minutes. Sprinkle with cheese, then return to the oven for a few minutes before serving. Serves 6.

CORN BARBECUE ROLLS

2 cups flour
¾ teaspoon salt
4 teaspoons baking powder
4 tablespoons shortening
1 egg, beaten
⅔ to 1 cup milk
1 can (12 oz.) whole kernel corn
Melted butter
Paprika

Mix the dry ingredients and work in shortening. Add beaten egg and milk; mix to a soft dough. Place on a floured board, roll to ½-inch thickness, spread with drained corn, and brush over with melted butter. Roll as for jelly roll and cut with a sharp knife into ½ to 1-inch slices. Place the slices, cut side down, on a cooky sheet, and dust with paprika. Bake in a 425° oven for about 15 minutes. Serve with country gravy, or simply as a bread with lots of butter. Makes 6 to 8 rolls.

FIREPIT COOKING

ON THE COALS

CHUCK ROAST

3 pounds chuck roast, cut 3 inches thick
1 clove garlic
1/4 cup olive oil
1/2 jar prepared mustard (approximately)
Salt

Put the meat in a flat pan or on a platter. Rub it thoroughly with garlic, then smear it with olive oil. Spread plenty of mustard on it, and pat in all the salt that will cling to it. Repeat on the other side. Let stand an hour or more.

Let your fire burn down until you have a deep bed of glowing coals. Gently place the meat right on the coals—no grill. Turn only once during cooking, and allow 20 minutes to a side for rare. To serve, slice the meat in strips. Serves 4 generously.

(Note: The oil and mustard absorb a considerable amount of salt, thus forming a coating which adheres to the meat. This salty crust prevents the meat from becoming charred and, in addition, keeps the juices inside.)

SALT STEAK

Wet and pack 5 or 6 pounds of rock salt around a 2- or 3-inch steak and place in paper sack. Salt coating must be at least 1-inch thick.

Bury in deep bed of glowing coals and leave 25 to 40 minutes. Break away salt crust and slice meat.

HAMBURGERS IN FOIL

Hamburger patties, sliced potatoes, and carrot sticks can be cooked together in a foil slipcover. Don't forget the salt, pepper, monosodium glutamate, and a layer of prepared mustard on the meat. This combination will require about 15 minutes of hot coal cooking.

STEAK ON FOIL

Steak is broiled on foil, not in it. Arrange the steak on a sheet of foil but do not wrap. Place directly on top of the hot coals and broil, turning once. The length of time required for broiling depends on whether you like rare or well done steak.

CAMP BAKED TROUT

- 1 12-inch trout
- 1/4 teaspoon salt
- 1/4 small onion, diced fine
- 1 thin strip bacon
- Maple leaves

Clean the trout and cut off the head and tail. Sprinkle the salt and the onion evenly inside the trout, then place the strip of bacon over the diced onion so that it will not fall out. The trout so dressed is then ready to be wrapped firmly with wet maple leaves, so that the entire surface is covered. The maple leaves will prevent the fish from sticking to the mud, and will prevent any loss of moisture from the meat. Make a mold of wet earth or clay 2-inches thick over the side and ends of the fish, patting the mud down solidly so that the fire can reach no portion of the meat. This mud must be wet enough to mold but not so wet that it will lose shape. After the fish is prepared in this manner, bury it in the red hot coals of the campfire. The fire should be raked back over the fish and kept burning slowly for one hour.

Then take the fish from the fire and break open the mud shell. The skin of the trout will stick to the maple leaves. The fish should then be split open and the backbone removed, and the trout is ready to be served. Serves 1.

MOLLUSKS—ROASTED

Clean and scrub shells thoroughly and place on coals. Serve with butter, salt and pepper.

FOILED FRUIT

You can manage campfire baked apples or bananas with the help of foil. To bake an apple, cut a slice off the top, remove the core, sprinkle a teaspoon of brown or white sugar in the hollow. Place on a square of foil and bring the corners up around the apple, twisting them together at the top to hold them secure. Bake 30 minutes. To bake bananas, simply wrap in foil, skin and all, and bake about 10 minutes on the coals.

LYONNAISE POTATOES

To cook lyonnaise potatoes: Cut a large potato and an onion into thin slices, mix, add a little salt and a bit of butter, wrap in foil, and cook for 15 minutes on the coals. Serves 2.

SHALLOW PIT BARBECUE

OPEN-PIT BARBECUE

Ordinarily the meat chosen for a barbecue of this type is a small pig, lamb or calf. Here are directions for cooking it:

Select first-class meat weighing from 35 to 50 pounds. Remove the head near the shoulders. Cut off the feet at the first joint. Saw the backbone through the middle lengthwise so that it will open out flat, but do not cut the carcass in halves. For lamb and veal cut off the thin flanks with a circular cut. Run sharpened iron rods or oak sticks lengthwise through the hams and shoulders just under the skin and under the ribs. This will permit the thick parts to come nearer to the fire for better cooking and, if the rods are run through in such a way as to support them, the ribs will not fall out when the meat is tender. These rods should be long enough to rest on the banks of the pit, and also to furnish hand holds for lifting and turning. Three or four smaller rods must be stuck through the sides at intervals and held to the main rod by hay wire. This prevents the tender cooked meat from falling off.

The pit should be 16 inches deep and as wide and long as needed to accommodate the meat. The hard wood fire should have been started several hours in advance of the cooking, to be burned down to a good bed of coals. At one end of the pit, away from

the meat, or in another pit, should be an auxiliary fire from which more coals can be added to the cooking fire as needed.

Place the meat over the fire, meat side down, until warm. Then turn meat side up and baste, using a large swab, with a strong solution of warm salt water containing a little cayenne pepper, and turn back again. The meat is cooked with the open side down, skin side up, during the first part of the cooking. A quart of salt will be needed for a 50-pound pig. Baste as often as the meat becomes dry, and repeat until the meat is nearly done. Then increase the heat by putting more coals under the thick sections of the meat. Then baste two or three times with plain warm water to wash the excess salt from the outside. At this point the meat should be carefully watched to prevent burning. When nearly done baste with the barbecue sauce (recipe given below). When done and very tender, remove some of the coals from the pit and turn skin side down to brown and crisp. While this is done the meat side should be basted frequently with salt water and barbecue sauce. (Remember to keep both salt water and sauce warm throughout the cooking.)

When carving to serve, put the skin pieces in one pan and the meat in another. Baste the meat with the barbecue sauce, but leave the skin pieces as they are, for basting makes them gummy instead of crisp and brittle as they should be.

Here's the recipe for the barbecue sauce to be used in the above procedure:

- 2 pounds butter
- 2½ quarts water
- 1½ tablespoons dry mustard
- ¼ cup sugar
- 3 tablespoons salt
- 3 tablespoons chili powder
- ½ teaspoon cayenne
- 2 tablespoons Worcestershire sauce
- 1 cup vinegar
- 2 teaspoons Tabasco sauce
- 3 tablespoons black pepper
- 4 tablespoons paprika
- 1 onion, chopped fine
- 1 clove garlic, minced

These ingredients are mixed and boiled together gently for 30 minutes before using.

SALMON BARBECUE

To begin with, get strictly fresh fish, and allow one pound "on the hoof" for each person to be served. Silver, Spring and Sockeye are the best varieties for the purpose. If the weather is warm, pack fish in ice until ready for use.

Start the fire four hours before serving time, on level ground. Choose a cleared spot away from any inflammable material. The fire should be long and narrow—1 foot wide and 3 feet long for the first one or two fish, then an additional 3 feet in length for every two more fish thereafter. Start it with anything handy, but feed it with half-dry alder poles. If no alder is available use any hard wood, such as vine maple or maple. In cooking, a slow steady fire should be maintained.

Frames against which the fish are supported during the process of barbecuing, are built by placing a rail the length of the fire (on both sides if more than a single salmon is to be barbecued) supported by stakes at each end. This rail should be about 2 feet from the fire and 18 inches above the ground.

Using a sharp knife, with plenty of water at hand, scale and clean the salmon in the usual manner. Then cut out the backbone by making an incision down each side of it on the inside (flesh side), being careful not to cut through the skin. After the backbone has been removed, the fish can be flattened out, flesh side up. It is in this position that two long wooden skewers, ½-inch in diameter, are thrust entirely through the body of the fish from side to side, about 12 inches apart. These should be long enough to project about 10 inches on either side. Then salt should be rubbed generously into the fleshy side of the fish.

Next the salted and skewered fish are stood against the rails, supported by the ends of the skewers, in a slightly slanting position. The flesh side must be toward the bed of coals. The cooking time now takes about 2½ to 3 hours, and all the cook can do is watch and keep the slow, even bed of coals going.

When the fish are thoroughly done, turn each one around so that the skin side is toward the fire and allow it to cook that way for a half hour longer. This adds much to the flavor by driving the oils, which have collected in the skin, back into the meat to keep it from being dry.

DEEP-PIT BARBECUE

The following plan is outlined to serve 20 people, but may be increased as many times as necessary to serve a really big crowd. When increasing amounts, remember never to put more than 25 pounds of meat in one bundle and never more than 8 bundles in one pit. Dig another pit if you're planning to feed more than 160 guests.

(NOTE: For a permanent pit such as shown in detail in the

"Sunset Barbecue Book," this same procedure may be followed. An alternative is to roast the meat unwrapped in the wire basket suspended in the center of the pit. The cleaned, skinned carcass may be roasted whole, without removing any bones, or it may be cut in portions weighing 40 to 50 pounds each and tied with heavy twine, like rolled roasts of beef. For this type of big barbecue allow one-half to one pound of meat for each person to be served.)

Take 25 pounds of meat—beef, mutton or venison—fairly fat. Lean venison can be used by putting in with it a pound or two of sliced bacon. Remove all bones and as many of the large sinews as possible. In doing this do not cut the meat into smaller pieces than is necessary. Season with ½ cupful of salt, ¼ cupful of black pepper, ¼ cupful sugar, and 2 tablespoons of garlic salt or 6 to 8 cloves of garlic. Rub the seasonings into the meat. Put in clove garlic by sticking a knife in the larger pieces and putting the cloves in the holes. Wrap the meat in two thicknesses of cheesecloth and sew up. Wrap this bundle in two thicknesses of burlap sacking and sew. Tie both ways with baling wire.

For the fire dig a hole 4 feet deep, 3 feet wide and 3 feet long. Increase the length by an additional 2 feet for every additional bundle of meat that you want to cook. Cover the bottom of the pit with a 6-inch layer of rocks. Lay the sides up with a rock layer of the same thickness to a height of 18 inches. Lay an iron rod across the top of this wall every 2 feet. Secure a piece of sheet metal that will fit close to the edges when put on these rods.

Build a fire of hard wood on the rocks under the rods. Start at least 4 hours before you want to put the meat in. Keep it burning just fast enough so that the flames rise a little above the rock wall. To fire faster is only a waste of fuel. When the fire has burned for 4 or 5 hours the rocks will be white hot and you can see through them. Let the fire drop a little. Take a rake or hoe and drag out any burning sticks, leaving just the coals.

Then drop in the bundles, being careful not to dislodge the rods. Put the sheet metal in place over the meat. Grab your shovels and throw the dirt in, beginning at the edges first. It is necessary to do this rapidly, for if the air is not shut out the heat of the pit will burn the meat up. Sixty seconds from the time the meat leaves your hand you should have at least a foot of dirt on top of the sheet metal. When finished, you'll have 3 feet of dirt over the metal.

The meat then must remain in the pit for at least 15 hours. No

harm is done if it's in for 24 hours. There is no need to watch after the first hour, during which time you must watch for escaping steam. This can be stopped by pouring a little water into the ground where it appears. It must be stopped or the heat escapes, and the meat doesn't cook.

PIT-ROASTED BEEF

This plan serves 10 guests. Dig a pit 3 feet long, 2 feet wide and about 2½ feet deep. The sides should slope in slightly toward the bottom. Line the bottom of the pit with six old bricks. Trim a piece of sheet metal slightly smaller than the top opening so it will fit into the pit to rest on the earth at the sides about halfway down.

Eight hours before you plan to serve, start a fire in the pit, on top of the bricks. (Pull the sheet of metal off to one side, out of the way.) Keep the fire burning briskly in order to fill the pit with live coals.

For the meat select a fine 12-pound rump roast. Stab it in several places with a narrow-bladed knife, and insert in each cut a thin sliver of garlic. Rub the outside of the roast with salt and pepper and wrap it in 4 or 5 thicknesses of wet cooking parchment and then in 4 or 5 thicknesses of wet burlap. Tie this in place with wire.

After about 3 or 4 hours, when the pit is full of glowing coals, scoop them out, exposing the hot bricks. Cover these with an inch or so of ashes or earth and drop in the bale of meat. (Be sure the burlap wrappings are thoroughly water-soaked.) Cover the bale with the sheet metal and shovel the coals back in on top. Add a stick or so of wood to the pile to keep them glowing, and leave them there for 4 hours.

At the end of that time shovel out the coals, lift the sheet metal away, and pull out the bale of beef. Use pliers to cut away the wire and pull apart the burlap wrapping. Unwrap the parchment paper carefully to save the pint or so of juice about the meat. Mix this with a little Worcestershire sauce and a half glassful of red or white wine and bring to a boil. It's a rare meat sauce.

IMU COOKERY

Prepare the fire pit by digging a hole about two feet deep, lining the bottom and sides with medium-sized stones. Do not use sandstone or wet rocks from a creek bed. Build a good fire of wood in

the pit, and put a few more rocks in it. When it burns down to coals, remove the extra rocks and the coals and save them for future use. Line the pit with fresh grass or leaves. If you use leaves, be sure that they are not bitter because this would impart an unpleasant flavor to your food. Taste them to be sure they are sweet.

Season your meat and wrap it securely in aluminum foil or plain wrapping paper. Do the same with your potatoes (either peeled or in their jackets, as you prefer), and other vegetables, wrapping them individually and securely. Carrots, turnips, onions, squash—all these and many others are delicious when cooked by this method.

Place your wrapped meat and vegetables on the bottom of the pit, cover with a thick layer of grass or leaves, and cover with the hot stones. Now replace the still hot coals on top of the stones. And, last, but not least, cover with the earth from the original excavation, making sure that it is airtight so that there is no steam or smoke escaping.

After three or four hours, depending upon the size and type of your meat, you are ready for a piping hot dinner, one that you will enjoy even more when you know that there are no pots and pans to wash!

TUNA LUAU

1 long fin tuna, about 25 pounds
1 stone lined pit, which has had a fire burning in it for at least 10 hours
12 large banana leaves. If not available, four clean wet gunny sacks
2 big bulbs of garlic, ground in food chopper
½ bottle Tabasco sauce
1 cup sugar
1 bottle Worcestershire sauce
½ cup prepared mustard
2 bottles catsup
½ pint vinegar
1 quart olive oil
½ gallon Sauterne
Salt and pepper

Do not clean the fish. Wrap the tuna in dampened banana leaves or wet gunny sacks. Place in a pit of hot stones, cover with ashes a foot deep, then place a layer of earth 6 inches deep over the ashes. After about 6 hours, build a fire of oak charcoal on top of the pit and let it burn down for about 3 hours. Combine the sauce ingredients and simmer for about 10 minutes, stirring constantly. Now you are ready to dig out the tuna. With a shovel, place the steaming tuna on a big wooden plank, peel off the wrappings and skin. Feed the innards to the dog or to any guests unappreciative of your efforts. The pieces of tuna are eaten Poly-

nesian style with the fingers, dipping the tuna into the bubbling sauce. Serve with dry white wine. Serves 15.

KING SALMON

To pit-barbecue a king salmon, first dig a 3-foot pit in the usual manner. A 40-pound king salmon will probably measure about 40 inches in length, so you'll need a pit 4 or 5 feet long, depending on the size of the fish. Build a fire of hardwood, and let it burn down until it forms a bed of coals 8 to 12 inches deep.

Meanwhile, place the fish on a large sheet of parchment, fill the stomach cavity with chopped onions, celery, and parsley. Squeeze lemon juice over the outside, and sprinkle all over with pickling spices. Then wrap it snugly in parchment, 3 or 4 layers of newspaper, and three gunny sacks. Fold the burlap neatly and wire in place with light wire.

Turn the hose on the package until the burlap and newspapers are soaked through. Place the bundle in a chicken wire sling and lower it into the pit on top of the coals. Cover with a piece of sheet metal, and shovel a foot of dirt on top of the covering. Build a small fire on the dirt, and keep burning until 1 hour before removing the fish. Cook 6 hours. A 40-pound king salmon will serve about 20.

KIPPERED SALMON

For kippering salmon, you will need a 4-foot-square open box, a piece of canvas, a joint of stovepipe with elbow, a stretch of sandy beach, and, of course, a few choice salmon.

Scoop out a shallow cavity in the sand and dig a trench in which to lay the stovepipe that provides draft to the fire. Build a fire of dry maple, and once it is burning readily, sprinkle it with sand and salt water to produce a heavy blue smoke. Place the open-ended box around the smoldering fire; arrange the salmon, filleted and cut in chunks, on a lath rack fitted into the box 10 inches below the top. To keep the smoke from escaping, fit boards tightly across the top, and throw a heavy canvas over all. From time to time, freshen the fire by poking additional fuel down the stovepipe.

After about 2 hours of continuous smoking, the salmon is ready to eat—rich and tender—á la Puget Sound Indian. Any fish that is not consumed on the spot may be kept for later. The smoking will make it last 3 weeks.

SALADS ON THE SIDE

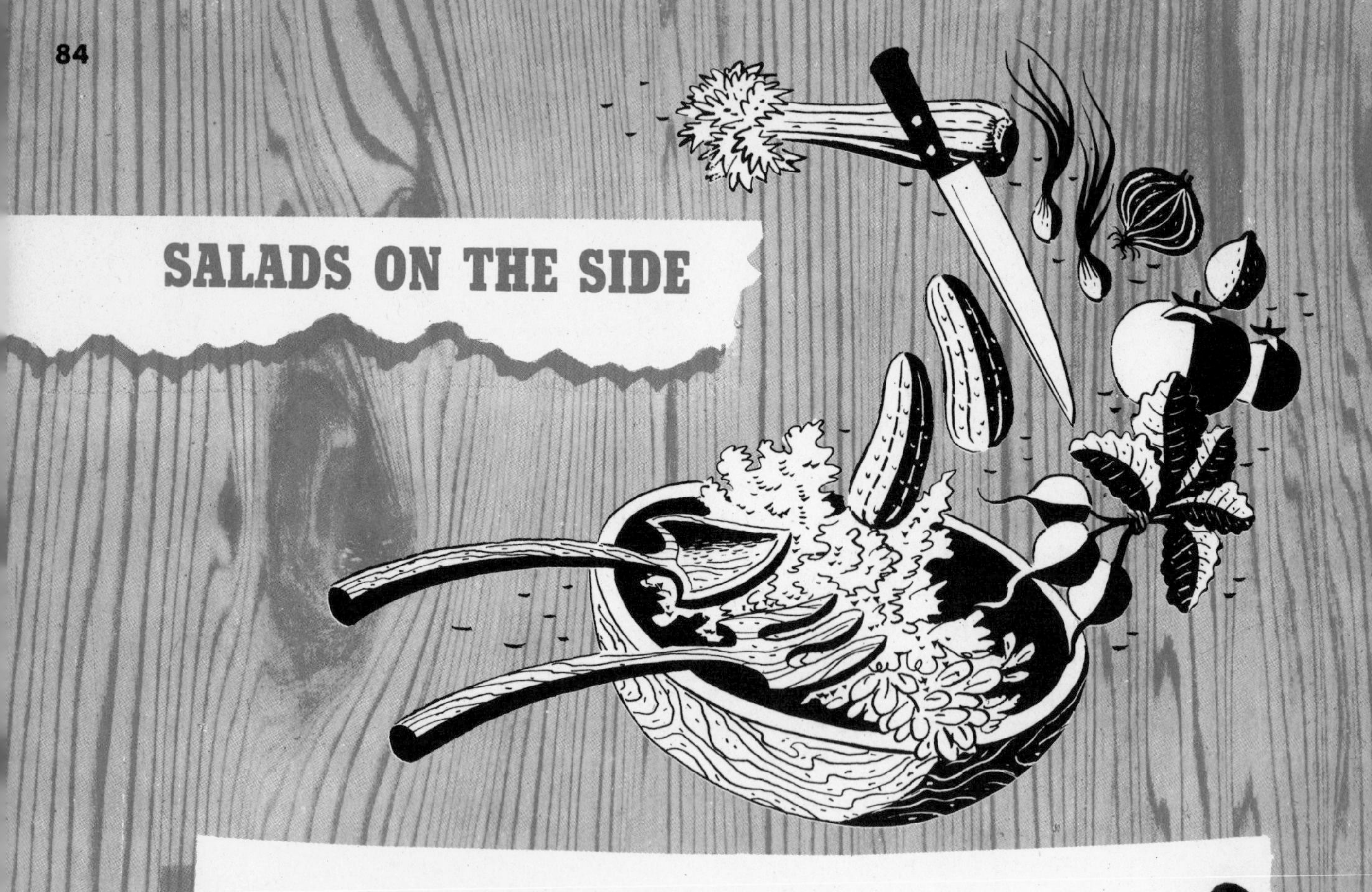

CABBAGE SALAD À LA MILLER

6 firm cabbages, shredded
6 medium onions, shredded
16 carrots (approximately), shredded
1 teaspoon celery seed
1 jar (8 oz.) sweet pickle relish
French dressing
Mayonnaise
Salt and garlic salt to taste

Mix vegetables, celery seed, and relish thoroughly, and marinate in French dressing for about 30 minutes. Drain and add mayonnaise to your liking, then season with salt and garlic salt to taste. Arrange in large bowl and garnish with chopped ripe olives, parsley, and paprika. Serves 30.

CAESAR SALAD

1 large clove garlic
4 small heads romaine
2 eggs, boiled 1 minute
3/4 cup grated Parmesan cheese
1 teaspoon Worcestershire sauce
1/4 cup olive oil
2 tablespoons tarragon wine vinegar
2 cups croutons, made from sour French bread
Salt and freshly ground pepper
Juice of 1 lemon

Mash garlic clove in salad bowl and rub around sides. Add romaine, torn in fairly large pieces. Mix in olive oil until each leaf is coated. Scoop the soft-cooked eggs out onto the greens. Add other ingredients, using lemon juice last. Toss well.

BARBECUE-SALAD DRESSING

1 cup salad oil
2 teaspoons salt
½ teaspoon paprika
½ teaspoon pepper
1 tablespoon prepared mustard
3 drops Worcestershire sauce
¼ cup tarragon vinegar
¼ cup cider vinegar
2 cloves garlic, cut in half

Mix thoroughly with a rotary beater. After allowing the garlic to impart its flavor, remove it.

About 30 minutes before broiling lamb chops or steaks, brush the meat liberally with some of this dressing. Then dip a swab of celery leaves in the dressing and baste the meat with it while cooking.

To what is left of the dressing, add ½ cup oil, and a dash of sugar, if desired, and stir vigorously. Pour it over crisp mixed greens for a simple tossed salad.

BASIC OIL AND VINEGAR DRESSING

¾ cup salad oil or olive oil
1 clove garlic, sliced lengthwise
¼ cup vinegar or lemon juice
1 teaspoon sugar
½ teaspoon salt
Freshly ground pepper
Paprika

Measure oil into fruit jar; add garlic and let stand for several hours. Remove garlic if only mild flavor is desired. Add remainder of ingredients, cover jar tightly and shake contents until well blended. Chill before using. Makes 1 cup dressing.

DRESSING FOR TOSSED SALAD

1 medium-sized onion, grated
3 cloves garlic, grated
1 tablespoon EACH salt, sugar, dry mustard, and crushed dry tarragon
½ teaspoon freshly ground black pepper
1 cup catsup
1 cup vinegar
2 cups oil

Mix together the onion, garlic, and seasonings in a quart jar. Pour in catsup, vinegar, and oil, and shake until thoroughly blended.

DRESSING IN QUANTITY

1 can (10½ oz.) condensed tomato soup
10½ oz. olive oil
10½ oz. red wine vinegar
2 onions, grated
Garlic to taste
Salt and pepper

Empty can of tomato soup into bowl, refill can with olive oil and pour into bowl, refill can again with the vinegar, and add to the tomato-oil mixture. Add quartered onions, garlic, salt, and pepper; blend ingredients. Let stand overnight and then remove onions.

GORGONZOLA DRESSING

- ¼ pound Gorgonzola cheese, crumbled
- 2 cloves garlic, chopped fine
- ¼ teaspoon salt
- ¼ teaspoon freshly ground pepper
- 1 tablespoon wine vinegar
- 1 tablespoon Worcestershire sauce
- 4 tablespoons olive oil

Combine all ingredients, and let stand in a warm place until flavors work through, stirring occasionally. This will make enough dressing for a salad for 4.

For variation: Mix in high-speed drink mixer to produce thick, creamy dressing.

GREEN SALAD WITH HERB DRESSING

- 1 cup salad oil
- 2 cloves garlic, cut in halves
- 2 tablespoons minced green onion
- 2 teaspoons each chopped fresh basil or tarragon
- 1 pinch crumbled rosemary
- 1 teaspoon salt
- ½ teaspoon coarse black pepper
- 2 tablespoons sugar
- ½ teaspoon dry mustard
- ⅔ cup wine vinegar
- 1 large head crisp lettuce
- 1 head romaine
- Watercress
- Few-sprigs parsley

Place salad oil into pint fruit jar. Drop cut cloves of garlic into oil and let stand for 2 or 3 hours. Remove garlic. To oil add onion, herbs, salt, pepper, sugar, and mustard. Pour vinegar in slowly, stirring well. Place cover on jar and shake to combine ingredients. Wash salad greens and tie in a damp cloth; keep cold. Just before serving, tear greens and place in a salad bowl. Toss lightly with the herb dressing. Serves 6.

MANDROS SALAD

- 1 clove garlic
- 1 head lettuce, torn
- 1 cucumber, diced
- 1 dill pickle, diced
- 1 large carrot, diced
- Stuffed olives, sliced
- 1 small can anchovies
- 1 can asparagus, or fresh equivalent, cut up, and cooked
- 6 or 7 radishes, sliced
- 3 stalks celery, sliced
- 3 green onions, sliced
- 1 pinch EACH of the following herbs: rosemary, oregano, sage, basil, thyme, marjoram and savory
- Olive oil
- Tarragon wine vinegar

Rub salad bowl with garlic. Put lettuce in first, then remaining ingredients in order listed. Dress the salad with olive oil and wine vinegar. Toss lightly. Garnishes may be hard-cooked egg slices, stuffed olives, asparagus tips, cucumber rings, slivered green beans, and radish roses.

FIESTA SALAD

1 cup mayonnaise
1 teaspoon chili powder
Dash of catsup or chili sauce
Dash of cayenne
Salt and pepper to taste
1 can (No. 2) unflavored red beans
1 cucumber, diced
1 small onion, finely chopped
1 bell pepper, diced
3 large tomatoes, diced
4 slices bacon, cooked and crumbled

Combine the mayonnaise and seasonings in a salad bowl. Add drained beans and other vegetables. Mix well and chill. Add the bacon at the last minute to retain its crispness. Garnish with lettuce before serving. Serves 6 to 8.

SMOKY SALAD DRESSING

½ teaspoon dry mustard
Dash of garlic oil
2 drops liquid smoke
Pinch salt
1 teaspoon soy sauce
1 tablespoon wine vinegar
½ teaspoon lime or lemon juice
3 tablespoons salad oil (delicate flavor of olive oil is lost in this blend)

Whip together with a fork, pour over torn lettuce, toss and serve.

TOMATO SALAD

Slice firm tomatoes into medium-thick slices and spread on a large platter. Anoint with a few drops of olive oil and wine vinegar, then sprinkle thickly with chopped herbs, parsley, chives, tarragon, basil, dill, and any others of your choice. Chill thoroughly. This salad can be made well in advance of the barbecue. Store in refrigerator.

TWENTY-FOUR-HOUR FRUIT SALAD

Here's a salad that teams up well with wild game, chicken, or grilled ham.

Juice of 3 lemons, grated rind of 1½ lemons
½ cup sugar
3 egg yolks, beaten
1 pint cream
1 can grated pineapple
1 pound Thompson seedless grapes
1 cup chopped walnuts
1 cup marshmallows

Cook lemon, sugar, and eggs in double boiler and cool. Whip the cream, mix with lemon custard, and work in the fruit and marshmallows. Let stand in refrigerator overnight.

HOW TO BARBECUE

The beginning barbecuer will be generously loaded down with instructions by his experienced friends. He has no need to be discouraged by their apparent expertness, for the techniques are easily mastered. The novice should have no trouble once he learns how to control his fire, how to use barbecue equipment, how to cook which kinds of meat, and how to plan a meal.

A barbecuer can surround himself with a formidable inventory of accessories. Here's the minimum list: large bib apron, asbestos gloves or half flour sacks for pot holders; long-handled spoon, fork, spatula; poker and ash shovel; clothes sprinkler; large skillet, Dutch oven, and a giant coffee pot.

THE BARBECUE FIRE

The beginning barbecuer often makes the mistake of trying to cook over open flame instead of waiting for coals to form. Only coals that have been allowed to burn to a gray color, shot with a ruddy glow, give the even, constant heat needed for barbecuing.

The distinctive flavor of barbecued meat comes less from the smoke of the burning fuel than from the singeing of the meat's surface and from the smoke that rises from the smoldering meat drippings.

If a wood-smoke flavor is desired, there are several ways of obtaining it. Liquid smoke may be included in the marinade or basting sauce. With skill, the meat may be grilled before the bed of coals has fully formed and while the fuel is still giving off some smoke; or wood that is slightly damp or green may be used. A few chips of aromatic wood or flavorsome leaves may be tossed on the coals just before the meat is removed from the grill. Favorite aromatic varieties are oak, hickory, bay, alder, myrtle, and the orchard woods, such as apple, lemon, orange, and cherry. Some kinds are too zestful—eucalyptus gives meat a medicinal flavor, pine imparts a turpentine taste.

CHARCOAL FUEL: Charcoal is obtainable in a choice of lump or briquet form. Briquets produce uniform heat, yield long-lasting coals, and burn without sparking. However, the lump style is cheaper and gives off a truer wood aroma than briquets.

A charcoal fire is prepared by arranging the pieces loosely on the grate, large chunks at the bottom, so air can freely circulate through them. A bed of 2 or 3 inches depth should do for most grill cooking, but a deeper layer is needed for sustained pit roasting. The charcoal should cover an area on the grate slightly larger than that occupied by the food on the grill above.

Paper and kindling will usually coax charcoal into flame, but sometimes more encouragement is needed. Pine chips or kindling sticks are effective, as are various inflammable liquids, such as alcohol, anti-freeze, kerosene, diesel fuel, white gasoline, or commercially-made lighter solutions. These solutions should be allowed to burn off completely, however, otherwise they may impart a disagreeable taste to the meat.

Once charcoal starts to burn, it will usually form cooking coals in 45 to 75 minutes, depending on the type and its dryness. When the bed of coals must be freshened, chunks are introduced around the edge, not the center. Hot coals left over after the grilling may be scooped into a metal container with a tight lid and saved for another day. Charcoal should be stored dry as it picks up moisture from the air.

WOOD FUEL: Although some barbecuers broil quite successfully over fire made with scraps of orange crate, apple box, or pieces of old flooring, most barbecue chefs stick to orthodox cooking woods. The hard woods—such as oak, hickory, madrone, manzanita, and maple—are best for barbecuing because they burn slowly and yield a lasting bed of coals. Soft woods—such as pine, poplar, redwood, chestnut, and elm—produce inadequate coals, if any, and may blacken the meat with a tarry soot. These varieties are useful, however, for starting hard wood burning and for open-flame cooking with skillet, kettle, or hot plate.

Compressed sawdust logs and briquets will provide a fine bed of coals quickly, but the coals are not long-lasting and tend to break up if raked around on the grate. The sawdust logs will form coals more quickly if chopped into 1-inch discs beforehand.

There are as many ways of building a wood barbecue fire as there are barbecuers. Accepted practice, however, is to load the firebox with ALL the wood needed for the bed of coals required, fire it up, and let it burn undisturbed until it forms coals, usually in 1 to 4 hours. Adding more wood during this period just delays formation of the coals. A wood fire can be freshened with chips, twigs, small branches, or pieces of charcoal.

FIRE CONTROL: The method of controlling the cooking temperature at grill-level depends upon the type of grill used. If the grill and grate are stationary, grill-level heat is regulated by adding fuel when the fire cools down, or scooping out coals, pushing them aside, or crushing them on the grate if the fire gets too hot. With an elevating grill or grate, cooking temperature is increased by bringing grill and coals close together, reduced by separating them.

After meat has been cooking for a short time, it will begin to drip molten fat into the coals. The volatile drippings catch fire and the flames will set the meat afire if it is too close to the coals. Some barbecuers contend that charring improves the flavor, but most cooks try to prevent it. This can be done by dousing flare-ups with a clothes sprinkler or with a water-soaked rag on a long stick, or by cranking the meat out of danger.

USING BARBECUE EQUIPMENT

GRILL: Any of the meats—steaks, chops, bacon, frankfurters, ham slices—that are usually broiled or fried on the kitchen range can be barbecued on the grill. Less tender cuts should be pounded or ground before grilling, otherwise they should be cooked underground by the pit method or with liquids in a skillet or kettle. The grill should be greased lightly before using to prevent meat's "freezing" to the hot metal.

HOT PLATE: Meats that can be cooked on the grill can also be broiled on the barbecue hot plate. The plate also doubles as a frying pan for eggs, pancakes, hamburgers, and sausage. Better than the grill for quick barbecuing, it can be used over open flame without waiting for coals. It should be allowed to warm up before using, then greased lightly.

SKILLET & KETTLE: Smart chefs use these to bring variety to the barbecue meal or for side dishes to cook along with the grilling meat. Mainly useful for frying breakfast or brunch delicacies, cooking stews and casseroles, and for liquid cooking of durable meats. Some skillet recipes can be converted to the grill by using the cooking sauce for baste.

SPIT: Any of the meats that usually are oven-roasted—leg of lamb, chicken, turkey, rolled roasts—can be barbecued on the spit. Length of time required is about the same as for kitchen roasting, although a spit located in the open, unprotected, requires longer time allowances. On a windy day, roasting with an unshielded spit will not be successful. A meat thermometer is helpful, but it should be inserted carefully so it doesn't rest against bone or the steel spit or locking tines.

SKEWERS: Innumerable combinations of meat and vegetables and or fruit, suitable either as main dishes or appetizers, can be broiled on the steel barbecue skewers. Skewer cooking often demands close attention to prevent the meat from catching fire and to insure evenly cooked vegetables or fruit. As it is sometimes a very smoky operation, it should not be tried when wind is likely to carry smoke into the dining area.

OVEN: Many barbecue ovens are suited only to warming bread and plates, but quite a few equal the cooking efficiency of the kitchen variety. A light metal portable type, rested on top of the grill, will take care of light baking and casserole cooking. Most of the oven recipes in this book are primarily kitchen projects that may be completed in the barbecue oven or in a kettle set on the grill or hung from the fireplace crane. Some recipes, such as those for spareribs, may be adapted to the grill or spit by using the roasting sauce for a baste; others may be baked in the coals by wrapping the meat in aluminum foil.

POINTERS ON MEAT

BEEF should be tops in quality, well marbled with fat, velvety in texture, fine in grain, and well aged.

Steaks are the most popular barbecue cut. The proper way to broil them is a matter of raging controversy. Many cooks like to broil them quickly, searing them over a hot fire or even slapping them on the coals. Other barbecuers prefer to broil slowly over a coolish fire. Recent research favors the slow school of broiling, but the beginner will probably want to try both techniques before choosing sides.

Ground beef is an ideal item for the beginner to practice on—and a memorable treat from the grill of an expert. It should not be too fat, but if it is too lean it will crumble and fall through the grill unless it is held together with a binder, such as egg. Ground shoulder makes about the juiciest hamburgers. A trace of marrow often improves flavor.

PORK in its processed forms—bacon, tenderized ham, sausage—is more welcome to the barbecuer than the unprocessed forms because it does not require the interminable cooking time that the fresh variety needs for safe eating (leg of pork takes 8 to 10 hours on a spit). Exception: fresh pork spareribs are a perennial backyard favorite that can be tastily broiled on the grill, spit, or skewers or roasted in the barbecue oven. Pork is loaded with fat and should be cooked over a low fire. Overhot coals cause the fat (and flavor) to cascade into the fire.

LAMB is a tender meat that is easily barbecued over coals. Almost any cut can be used. Cubes sliced from shoulder or leg provide the basic ingredient of most shish kekab recipes. Cooking time is about the same as indoors. Heat requirements are for medium coals. Barbecued lamb should be served HOT as its fat congeals rapidly in the open air.

FOWL can be deliciously broiled on either the grill or the spit, but as most varieties are naturally dry, they tend to burn or dry out over the parching heat of barbecue coals. Their juices can be conserved, however, by marinating in an oil-base mixture before grilling, cooking over a cautiously managed fire, and basting frequently during the roasting period. Half fowl should be broiled skin-side down so the juices can collect in the cavity. Elderly birds are best cared for in the skillet or Dutch oven where they can be cooked in liquids that reduce their rubbery qualities.

FISH, like fowl, are usually short on fat, and what little they have is so volatile that it vaporizes over coals that are too hot. By wrapping them with some fat in leaves (maple or any sweet variety) or aluminum foil, the barbecuer can keep them juicy. Fish also tend to stick to the grill, even one that is well greased, and they are easier to turn and handle if placed in a wire toasting rack.

SAUCES AND MARINADES are used to sharpen the flavor of meats, fowl, or fish. There is no mystery about their composition. They are simply a blend of oil, seasonings, and a food acid such as lemon juice, vinegar, wine, or tomato juice. Some cooks believe that the acids help to tenderize meat. The amount of oil used varies according to the natural amount of fat in the meat.

BARBECUE MENUS

Because of the casual nature of the barbecue meal, selection of foods is a free-and-easy matter. In general, foods should be chosen that stand up outdoors (gelatine won't), that are easy to prepare and simple to eat —preferably with the fingers. Desserts that carry their own dishes, such as melons, bananas, fruit tarts, ice cream cones, save clean-up afterward. A good salad goes with any barbecue.

Suggested menus are on the following pages.

SUGGESTED MENUS . . .

OLD STANDBY

Hot Bouillon
Barbecued Steak (or Chops)
Potato and Onion Fries Hot Garlic Bread
Garden Salad Bowl
Fresh Fruit Pie Cheese
Coffee

SUPPER WITH A ROAST

Tomato Clam Bouillon
Spit Roast of Beef Barbecue Sauce
Scalloped Potatoes with Cheese
Buttered Green Beans Buttered Soft Rolls
Dill Pickles and Olives
Cantaloupe Halves
filled with Pineapple and Berries
Coffee Gingersnaps

STEAK SUPPER

Hot Bouillon or Iced Tomato Juice
Barbecued Steaks
Baked or Scalloped Potatoes
Garden Salad Bowl
Garlic French Bread "Finger Relishes"
Fresh Fruit au Naturel Lots of Hot Coffee

PIT-BARBECUE SUPPER

Pit-Roasted Beef Mexican Beans
Toasted French Bread
Tossed Salad with French Dressing
Monterey Cheese Fresh Fruit
Red Wine Coffee

GARDEN BARBECUE SUPPER

Barbecued Racks of Lamb
Roasted Corn on Cob
Hashed Brown or Scalloped Potatoes
Sliced Tomatoes Sliced Onions
Cole Slaw Pickles
Hot French Bread Coffee with Dinner
Iced Melons, Assorted Kinds

GARDEN BREAKFAST WITH LAMB CHOPS

Fresh Fruits in Season
Lamb Chops Griddle Cakes
Plum Butter Honey
Coffee

DINNER ON A SPIT

Hot Chicken Broth
Spit-Roasted Boned Leg of Lamb
Scalloped Potatoes and Cheese
Buttered Slivered Green Beans
Hot Buttered Rolls Radishes Olives
Chilled Fruit Cup
Caramel Squares Coffee

SUNDAY BARBECUE BREAKFASTS

I

Chilled Melon Wedges
Grilled Ham Fried Eggs
Hot Coffee Cake Doughnuts
Coffee

II

Prepared Cereal with Fresh Berries
Little Sausages Griddle Cakes
Coffee

HOMESPUN DINNER

Oven-Barbecued Spareribs Baked Beans
Cole Slaw Hot Cornbread
Apple Pie Cheese
Coffee

LAMB CHOP AND SALAMI GRILL

Scalloped Corn
Baked Tomatoes
Broiled Lamb Chops and Salami Slices
Heated Rolls
Tray of Fruit and Cheese Coffee

FINGER MEALS

I

Barbecued Rib Lamb Chops
or Spareribs
Saratoga Chips
Salad Platter: Raw Carrot Strips,
Caulifflowerets, Celery, Olives,
Pickles, Green Onions
Small Tomatoes, etc.
Cheese and Crackers   Beer

II

Fried Chicken
Shoestring Potatoes
Corn on the Cob
(Melted butter in bowl with brush)
Raspberry Tarts   Iced Coffee

HAMBURGER FEED

I

Barbecued Hamburgers
Picnic Buns   Canned Shoestring Potatoes
Cole Slaw   Sour Cream Dressing
Frosted Chocolate Cookies   Fresh Fruit
Coffee

II

Cole Slaw over Sliced Tomatoes
with Sour Cream Dressing
Grilled Hamburgers   Picnic Buns
Barbecue Sandwich Sauce
Saratoga Chips   Bread and Butter Pickles
Peach Turnovers   Chilled Milk

III

Broiled Hamburger Patties
Sliced Tomatoes and Onions
Potato Salad
Strawberry Shortcake with Cream
Coffee

SHISH KEBAB SUPPER

Sliced Tomato and Cucumber Salad
Shish Kebabs   Roasted Corn
Grilled Slices of Pineapple
French Rolls   Butter
Peach Shortcake   Coffee

MEATLESS MENU

Spanish Style Beans
Cheese Omelette
Avocado, Tomato and Lettuce Salad
French Rolls
California Burgundy

BARBECUED SALMON

Barbecued Salmon
Creamed Potatoes and Chives
Cabbage Salad with Sliced Tomatoes
Chopped Pickle Relish
Assorted Ice Cream Cups   Small Cakes
Coffee

SALMON SUPPER

Cheese-Frosted Biscuits
Broiled Salmon Steaks with
Lemon Wedges
Canned Shoestring Potatoes, Heated
Tossed Green Salad
Watermelon   Iced Tea

HAM SUPPER

Grilled Ham Steaks
or
Barbecued Spareribs
Tomatoes and Zucchini au Gratin
Hot Apple Sauce   Shoestring Potatoes
Corn Bread
Butter, Mustard Pickles, Tomato Jam
Sliced Peaches, Figs and Melon Balls
with
Raspberry Sauce
Coffee   Fruit Punch

OUTDOOR FIREPLACE MENU

Chilled Apple Juice
Lamb Stew with Fresh Vegetables
Hot Biscuits   Spiced Peach Butter
Sliced Cucumber Pickles
Orange-filled Layer Cake
Coffee

ROAST TURKEY DINNER

Spit Roasted Turkey   Celery Stuffing
Scalloped Potatoes
Fresh Vegetable Salad Bowl
Mixed Sweet Pickles   Cranberry Sauce
Assorted Rolls, Buttered and Heated
Apple Pie   Coffee

HAM DINNER

Broiled Ham Slice
Baked Sweet Potatoes
Baked Apple Quarters
Hot Garlic-Buttered French Bread
Cabbage Salad   Coffee

CHICKEN BARBECUE

Chilled Loganberry Nectar
Barbecued Chicken   Grilled Corn
Hot Buttered Rolls   Fresh Fruit Salad Bowl
Fresh Peach Freezer Ice Cream
Coconut Layer Cake
Coffee

BUFFET CART SUPPER

Shish Kebab
Mixed Green Salad with Avocado,
Mushrooms, and Cucumbers
Sesame Seed Rolls   Steamed Rice
Butter, Fig Jam, Green Olives, and
Pickled Peppers
Deep Dish Apple Pie
or
Peach Cobbler
Coffee   Milk

QUANTITIES FOR 24

Here are the quantities you will need to entertain 24 guests at your barbecue, average servings:

Bread	3 loaves
Butter	1 lb.
Beverages	
cider, grape juice	3 qts.
coffee	1½ lbs.
lemons (lemonade)	1½ doz.
oranges (juice)	3 doz. med.
milk	1¼ gals.
tomato juice	1 can (No. 10)
Cheese	
bulk	2½ lbs.
cottage	4¼ lbs.
Cream (coffee)	1 pt.
Fish	8 lbs.
Fruits, Canned	3 cans (No. 2½)
Fruits, Fresh	
apples (for pie)	8 lbs. (4 9-in. pies)
bananas	8 lbs.
cranberries	1½ lbs.
grapes	3 lbs.
pineapple	2½ pineapples
Ice Cream	4 qts.
Jams, Jellies	3 glasses (10 oz.)
Meat	
steaks or chops	12-16 lbs.
roasts	14-18 lbs.
spareribs	24 lbs.
Olives	
green	1 bottle (20 oz.)
ripe	4 cans (No. 1)
Poultry	12 lbs.
Salad Dressing	
French	3 bottles
mayonnaise	1½ pints
Soup (opening course)	4½ qts.
Sugar (cubes)	½ lb.
Vegetables, Canned	1 can (No. 10)
Vegetables, Fresh	
asparagus	8-9 lbs.
beans, string	6 lbs.
beans, lima	10-11 lbs.
beets	7 lbs.
broccoli	9 lbs.
cabbage, cooked	7 lbs.
cabbage, raw	4 lbs.
carrots	6 lbs.
cauliflower	14-15 lbs.
celery	5 hds., med.
lettuce	8-10 hds.
onions	6-7 lbs.
peas in pod	12 lbs.
potatoes, sweet	10 lbs.
potatoes, white	8 lbs.
squash	12 lbs.
tomatoes	7 lbs.

INDEX

(NOTE: This index covers recipes only.)